UNLIKELY
LOVE
STORIES

ALSO BY MIKE McCARDELL

Chasing the Story God
Back Alley Reporter
The Blue Flames that Keep Us Warm
Getting to the Bubble
The Expanded Reilly Method
Everything Works
Here's Mike

UNLIKELY LOVE STORIES

Mike McCardell

HARBOUR PUBLISHING

Harbour Publishing Co. Ltd.
P.O. Box 219, Madeira Park, BC, V0N 2H0
www.harbourpublishing.com

Cover photograph by Nick Didlick
Edited by Ian Whitelaw
Cover design by Anna Comfort O'Keeffe
Text design by Mary White
Printed and bound in Canada

Harbour Publishing acknowledges financial support from the Government
of Canada through the Canada Book Fund and the Canada Council for
the Arts, and from the Province of British Columbia through the BC Arts
Council and the Book Publishing Tax Credit.

Library and Archives Canada Cataloguing in Publication

McCardell, Mike, 1944–
    Unlikely love stories / Mike McCardell.

ISBN 978-1-55017-563-9

    1. Love—Anecdotes. 2. Love—Humor. 3. Interpersonal relations—
Anecdotes. 4. Kindness—Anecdotes. I. Title.

BF575.L8M42 2012   302.3   C2012-904285-4

This is dedicated to you. Yes, you. You have stuck by me. You have watched and listened and read. Without you I would not have had these stories. And without you I would have no one to tell them to.

So, please, write your name or the name of the person you are giving this to right here:

Thank you. I appreciate that more than you could guess. That will make two of us feel good, maybe three: you and me and someone else.

Contents

Introduction

Hello.

That may not be an orthodox way to begin a book, but I know you. You have been reading my books and watching me for a long time and I am pretty sure I think a bit like you and feel about things a bit like you and want and like things like you. That makes us friends, even if we haven't met. Sometimes I see you on the street. You say hello. You write to me. You often say nice things, which makes me feel good.

Of course there are tens of thousands of you who don't write and whom I never meet. If I were reading someone else's words and watching them on television I would never write to them. That's their job, I would think. They write, I read, even if I read slowly. They put stuff on television, I watch.

I go to work fixing shoes or selling stocks or teaching kids or protecting the country and I don't expect anyone to write to me so I don't write to them.

You are my kind of people.

So are you who do write.

I could not have a better life and it is time to write again and raise some more money for a good cause and give me one more chance to tell you the stories behind the stories that I find and, more than that, to tell you how they changed my life and how they can do the same for you.

Consider this a letter or an email; a love letter, not a book. Did you see the story about the woman I saw on a park bench who was writing a letter with a pen? I was stunned.

"Hello"—usual stuff. "You are using a pen?"

She said that writing that way, with ink, a method that is headed for extinction, was therapy for everything. It was relaxing and she could think about what she wanted to say. She felt good. It was less hectic than moving your thumbs over microscopic keys.

She writes to a couple of pen pals. She has been doing so since high school. But she also writes to someone in prison.

Oh, my gosh. That is the kind of thing I hope to hear. Someone doing something that is really different. Someone helping someone else.

"But I would not want that broadcast."

Oh, my darn gosh. The best part of the story and she does not want it told.

I cannot betray a confidence. I cannot take her picture and go away and later when she is not around say she is writing to someone behind bars. But I am aching while I talk to her. I want to hear about the person in prison but I am talking about the beauty of writing with a pen.

I can only talk about her secret kindness and her modesty now that her name and her picture on the screen are in the past. Stories are like that. Family stories are like that. They leave out a lot. You cannot talk about Aunt Ronnie because she was a prostitute. You cannot mention that your father would yell at your mother if Ronnie came by for a visit, and he would get out the Lysol and scrub the bathroom. Aunt Ronnie was probably a neat woman, but you cannot mention her, ever, unless you sneak her into a story.

I say story, but really that is just the trade name for the way we package an event. What has changed my life is not the stories, but the people who make the stories. It could have been Aunt Ronnie, if ever she could be mentioned, but it has certainly been people like you, and you, and you way over there watching a little league baseball game while carrying a 9mm pistol at your side, who have given me everything I want in life.

I bet the pistol story grabbed you. That is what writers do. They try to sneak one in just before you fall asleep. That will come later, but it is you, like the policeman watching the game on his lunch break, that make me know life is worth living.

But first I have to tell you I almost died while I was thinking about this.

I was on a shaky ladder 20 feet above the ground. Half of you do not know what 20 feet is. All the time I was growing up, 20 feet meant you would die if you fell that far. I have no idea what dying is in metric, and if you put 20 feet into the way we now do things, falling 6.096 metres has no meaning. I might not die.

How can the change of a word change the meaning of being way up high on a ladder? I was having great thoughts up there. I thought of you and of writing my meaning of life to you, and then I suddenly thought if I were to die the story would say I fell 6.096 metres, and even in my coffin I would not be impressed. Words change everything. Words are weird.

The laurel I was trimming was planted to hide my neighbour's hot tub. Then the neighbour moved. The new people took out the hot tub. The laurel stayed and grew. Some people say laurels are weeds on steroids. They are right.

I was snipping the top of the bush, which is crazy. When I was small there were no bushes for us to trim, and the only ladders were used by burglars. If my friends could see me now they would ask, "Are you trying to break into an apartment at the top of the tree when there are no apartments at the tops of trees? You have gone crazy."

Then the ladder slipped and as you can imagine, because you have been on a ladder that slipped, the first word out of my mouth was a bad word, a really bad word. And then the ladder stopped. I thought I had almost died, and if the ladder hadn't stopped I would have died. And if I had died, the last word out of my mouth would have been a bad word, a super-bad word.

I do not want that to happen. I don't know why I don't want that to happen—I do not believe I am going to a heaven, so a bad word does not make any difference—but I have learned to enjoy living so much that it would be a real bad thing to end it with a downer of a word.

And then I thought (all this I was thinking while still swaying at the top of a laurel 20 feet up) what have I learned from all this living?

I have learned that everything turns out well, if you want it to. And that you can be any kind of person you want to be, if you want to be that.

(I am thinking this while the ladder is slanted way over to one side and has hooked itself onto a branch that is stronger than my weight.)

And I have learned that getting angry is as dumb as punching yourself in the eye. And I've learned that letting other people be who they are is the only way to get along with other people.

This is not just chicken feed. This is powerful stuff. And I learned it all from meeting other people and talking to them and doing stories about them.

I realized this would not be an opportune time to die, and I climbed down so I could tell you about the baseball fan with the gun, and other nice stories.

First Real Story

'll start with the most touching moment of last year for me.

You'll remember the last book had the best dedication ever, EVER, in the history of books. It was, as you know, unplanned. It was a surprise even to me. It was to a woman whom I had never met who had breast cancer. I learned about her from her daughter who is a clerk in a liquor store. I was buying wine.

She asked me when I was going to write another book, and I told her never because I did not believe anyone read them. She said her mother did, and they gave her comfort.

In the next nanosecond I thought "How can my stories give anyone comfort? They are just stories of … of what? They are stories of ordinary things that just happen, and I look for them happening. Stories of an old fellow writing poetry to his wife and stories of crocuses coming up in the spring."

Nice stories, but comfort?

Yes, comfort, she said. So I said I would write another book. And I did. And I dedicated it to a woman named Judy.

At one of the book signings, at Black Bond Books in White Rock, a woman stood in line and when I asked her name she said, "Judy."

Then I asked, because that is what you do at a book signing, "Is this for you or someone else as a present?"

"It's for me, and I am Judy."

I lifted my pen and touched the first page of the book.

I started to write: "Dear Judy…"

Then my hand stopped.

Judy?

"Did you say Judy?"

"Yes."

Judy. She said Judy. And I knew, of course I knew. How could anyone be so stupid as to not know that this woman who had just said she was Judy was actually Judy.

"Judy?" I said.

And she smiled. The smile of someone who has just told a great secret that changes the world, like "I'm going to have a baby," or "I'm getting married," or "I know what you did last night." She says she is Judy and she knows that her name, that two-syllable name, will tell me her story.

"THE Judy?" I said.

She nodded.

I put down the pen and we hugged. Right there, in the book store, with a line of people who wanted books signed standing behind her, we hugged.

"This is Judy," I said to the lineup. "Stop, right now and if you have not done it, read the introduction."

A few of them said they had already read it. "Be patient," I said to them. "If you have read it, be patient. If you haven't, read it. Now."

Heads went down, then heads came up from the books. The faces of some had a hint of glistening about the eyes, and I said:

"This is Judy."

One person started clapping. Then another, and another. It was not applause. Applause is what happens after a performance on stage and you appreciate what the actors have done. This was clapping in honour of someone, in the realization that someone pretty amazing was standing in front of them. Someone who had survived cancer, like so many. Someone who had been scared and branded by death, but had come out alive.

Judy's face was one endless smile. Her eyes were dripping with tears.

When I sign books I stand next to a table. I never sit because I figure if you are standing while you wait for me to sign my name, I will stand while I do it. Besides, I hate to go into the boss's office and he is always sitting and you are always standing. So I stood, and now we who were two became one figure. It is what happens when you hug someone.

All teenagers, especially girls, hug when they meet, but I have watched them and that is not hugging. That is formula front-end almost touching. There was no almost with Judy and me. We hugged. We shared one space. There was no holding back. I felt her tears on my face.

That is the way life happens. You hear about someone, you talk about them, and later, accidentally or not, you meet them and at that moment you are in an actual sense, born again. You become better.

I signed the book. I don't remember what I said but I'm sure it was okay because I give everyone a personal message. Tell me something about yourself or about the person you are giving the book to, and I write something based on that.

For Judy, I did not have to ask.

She said she had a double mastectomy and was now doing fine.

I never saw her again. She wrote to me once on my email at work and sent me a picture of the two of us at the book signing that some-one had taken, but that was it.

That was the whole story. That is the only kind of story I under-stand. The kind that are real. They are not blockbusters or deep think-ing stories. They are stories that everyone has.

The stories in this book are yours. They are Judy's. They happen to you. Or they could happen to you. You will recognize the characters. They are your neighbours, or your kids, or you.

And, like magic, you never know when you'll get another story, because you never know when you will run into a Judy.

The Beginning
(which happened before I met Judy)

Before I met Judy I told myself the next book had to be different. I wanted something so novel it would knock your socks off.

For seven books I have told you about the stories behind the stories, like *Getting to the Bubble*. That was an amazing tale, at least to me. We went through a jungle of adventures before finding a little girl trying to teach her much younger sister how to blow bubbles.

It was a beautiful story and it started an entire book, but now I wanted to write something different. I wanted to write about the great thoughts that people can think. I wanted to look at something in a way that would make your head spin.

And so I wrote and wrote and wrote—more than 20,000 words. That's a lot of words. That's almost a quarter of a book. And then I put my head on the keyboard and went thump. I discovered I have a problem.

I have no great thoughts. And I see things the way I always have. I see only what is in front of me and I jot down what I see. And then I tell it.

This is what I told you to do in my last book. Just look for something funny or weird or happy or sad (not too much sad) and tell someone about it. Then the person you are telling the story to will have a better life just because you told him or her something that you thought was neat, and you will have a better life because you made someone else's life better. This is not a bad way to spend a day, or a life.

But me? No. That wasn't good enough for me. I wanted to do something else. I wanted to write about the mysteries of life. I wanted the deep thoughts. I wanted a blockbuster.

Then I met a man in a grocery store lineup and he said, "You did a story about my daughter. She was blowing bubbles. It made us feel so good."

The little girl, who was now much bigger, was packing away groceries. She was ignoring me. I don't blame her. She was so young she did not remember being on television. But her father did. One little story about blowing bubbles and he will talk about it for the rest of his life. One moment of surprise and delight and, believe me, it was funny. Watching this girl, who was sitting in a stroller and wasn't old enough to know how to blow her nose, much less how to blow through a plastic circle filled with soapy water, could make someone heading to the electric chair laugh.

Luckily, we have no more electric chairs, but we do have bubbles, and I realized in that grocery line that it is the little stories that are the blockbusters. And it is the little stories that I love.

We don't have to be different. We just have to be who we are and do what we love doing. You are you doing what you do. No one else can do it like you. You are living your life as best you can and that is the real story.

We are not Harry Potters. We are real, and these are real stories. Your stories.

And Then ... There's Nothing to Eat

I was working with someone who does not hold a phone to his ear when driving. The voice of the caller comes out of the speaker on the dashboard.

This was good for me. Not so good for his teenage daughter.

Ring.

"Hello," said my friend.

"Should I take the dogs out to pee?"

Pause.

I am thinking, but of course. Do you have to ask? Do they have to pee? Of course they have to pee. We all have to pee. Do you have to pee? Would you like someone asking someone else if you should be allowed to pee?

"Yes, that would be a good idea," said my friend to the dashboard.

From the dashboard came a sigh.

Pause.

"Alright, I'll take them out," said the dashboard.

"She's sixteen," said my friend.

A while later, just after enough time for two dogs to empty their bladders, which apparently were full because it was a while later, *Ring*.

"Hello."

"There's nothing to eat," said the dashboard.

"Take something out of the refrigerator," said my friend.

Sigh. It came from the speaker, which usually has music or news. Now, just *Sigh*.

This was not a quiet sigh. It was a sigh that said, "You don't understand. All I want is something to eat and you don't understand."

"There's nothing in the refrigerator," said the dashboard.

"Oh, come on, there must be something in there," said my friend.

We heard the breath inhaling, followed by the slight pause, then a long *Sigh*. It came out in A flat. This was a much louder, more pronounced sigh than earlier.

"There's nothing in there but ketchup and mustard and that other stuff you put on food."

"Your mother is shopping now. Take some eggs, I know we have eggs. Make yourself an egg sandwich."

Sigh.

"They're so messy."

"Well then there's tuna. We have cans of tuna. You always like the tuna sandwiches I make."

Sigh. It was the kind that meant, "I would have to open a can and then put the tuna on a slice of bread and then put some of your despicable mayonnaise on the tuna and then put another slice of bread on top of that and then I would have to eat it. *Sigh*."

"Never mind," said the dashboard. "Goodbye."

That was followed by a silence that filled the car.

"Like I said, she's sixteen," said my friend.

There is no punch line to this. I would love to tell you that later, when she heard I had been listening to the conversation, she said, "Oh, no. How could you do this to me? I am so embarrassed I will never complain again."

But when she learned I was listening she said, "Did he understand me?"

"No," said my friend.

Sigh.

You Can't Say That!

There are many problems newspapers and TV stations and people face. Mostly they concern words.

Suppose you are an editor in the *New York Times* newsroom. A young reporter comes to you and says she has the best story ever.

"Yes?" you say. But you don't mean yes. You mean what are you going to tell me that I have not heard a hundred times before but that you think is new?

Young reporters get carried away and think everything is the best story ever.

"Steamed balls," she says.

"Like in an Asian dish?" you ask.

"No, as in sweaty guys, playing handball."

Remember, this is the nation's most prestigious newspaper. It does not write about sweaty guys with steamed balls. In fact it does not even allow those words inside the newsroom. You might hear them in the press room if a giant roll of newsprint fell on someone's toes. Actually, you would hear other, worse things. But not in the newsroom, where they print, according to their masthead, all the news that is fit to print.

I've always wondered who decides what's fit. Most of the news organizations I have worked for print all the news that fits. When they run out of space or time they stop.

However, this young woman reporter, named Sarah Maslin Nir, said she had a story about steamed balls. The *Times* always uses the reporter's middle name, or at least initial. It makes them sound more prominent than reporters without middle names.

She explains to the editor that people, mostly men, who play handball have figured out a way of keeping their balls bouncing during the winter.

"They bring propane stoves and pots of water and steam their balls," she said.

This bit of urban news entered the newsroom while the editor was dealing with Republican and Democrat politics and the issues of the Supreme Court and the stock market.

"Really," the editor said, or at least I imagine he said that, since I have dealt with editors for most of my life and when they are stumped they often say, "Really?" It is said both with and without a question mark at the same time, which is why they are editors. They can do mystical things with words.

"Really," said Sarah. "They put their balls in the pots and steam them. Then they can bounce better. Do you know how bad it is to have cold balls?"

I was not there, but I know her editor looked at her over his glasses and said exactly nothing. He did not even shake his head. There is no way he was going to answer that question, not from a young girl who was excited about telling him of her discovery of steamed balls.

She went on:

"When it gets cold their balls don't bounce as well."

This is not news to half the world.

"So they have to warm up their balls," she said. "And how do you do that in a public space?"

Again, the editor did not answer. That has been a problem, he knew, since long before this girl was born.

"Well now I know and I can write a story about it," she said.

He could only manage one raised eyebrow. Anything else would have him answering questions to the human rights committee of the newspaper.

Handball, as everyone in New York knows, is the national sport of New York. That is because all you need is a ball and a wall and New York has more walls than just about any other place on earth outside of Vancouver's West End.

If you do not know what handball is, I will explain. In Vancouver, everyone who is not jogging or doing yoga plays tennis. If they do not have a partner they hit a ball against a wall with a racquet and then hit again. Handball is the same, without a racquet but with someone else, someone who knows about steamed balls.

Two people stand side by side and hit a ball against a wall. Many of them are good. Some are very good. This is their only sport and they have played it all their lives. The ball can be driven so fast you can barely see it. Sometimes there are four players.

Everyone in New York grows up playing this. Yes, everyone. When you are young you eat bagels and play handball. When you get older you eat bagels and watch others play. There are 5,000 outdoor official handball courts in the city, plus a million other unofficial walls of buildings that make do for a temporary court. The nearest city to that is Los Angeles, which has 500 courts.

But when it gets cold the balls contract and do not bounce as well as warm balls. This is a universal truth.

"So some guys have been setting up their heaters at the back of the courts," said Sarah. She had seen this herself, which is the sign of a good reporter, finding things that are happening to report on.

"And they steam their balls," she said. "Then they bounce better."

The editor knew any story about handball would make it into the paper. Even the *Times* cannot reject stories of immense popularity. But the mention of steamed balls would not enter into it. The editor knew that the next day everyone in New York would be talking about the story of the steamed balls. And then they would say it was in the *New York Times* and they would smirk. Smirking is not encouraged by the *Times*.

But editors, as I always say, since they have fixed up my words for fifty years, are smart.

"Okay, write it," he said.

She wrote. Then the editor edited.

The headline: "In Queens, Cold Weather Brings Heat to Handball."

In a twenty-two-paragraph article, the words "steamed balls" never appear. "Steam ball," the singular version, is seen once inside a quote from one of the players, and this variation on the game is referred to as "steamball." The story mentions the circumference of the balls, just under two inches, and their weight, sixty-one grams. It explains how the water is boiled with propane heaters. But the idea or suggestion that the game is made better with steamed balls is never written and never read.

I talked to a friend in New York the next day. He said his friends were all laughing about this great story in the *Times*. "It was so funny. It's all about how you can play with steamed balls on a cold day. I never would expect that in the *Times*," he said.

Another truth in life: No matter what is said or written, you hear and read what you want to hear and read.

Polka Dot Joe

"Grandpa, can you help me catch a ladybug?"

Well, of course. Nothing could be easier than catching a ladybug. If granddaughter asked for the most difficult thing on earth it would take a little longer, but a ladybug will take only a few minutes.

Anyone can catch a ladybug. They don't crawl very fast. And if you put your finger in front of one she will probably climb right on board. Then you can put her into a jar and say, "Look, granddaughter, here's a ladybug."

And then you wait for the words, "Grandpa, you can do anything."

And then, again, life is beautiful.

"Why do you want a ladybug?" I asked.

"So I can keep him in a house I made and call him Polka Dot Joe."

"But aren't ladybugs ladies?"

"Not Polka Dot Joe. He's a special ladybug."

"How will you know when you find it that it's the right one?"

"I'll know," she said.

The single best thing about grandchildren is you can discover the world for the first time. We all know that when you were a kid you worked in a coal mine or up a chimney or delivered newspapers all day long. That is what you told your kids, so it must have been true.

"When I was a kid we didn't have these kinds of toys like G.I. Joe or Raggedy Ann. No sir, we had clothes pins, and then only on the days when my dear Momma was not washing, and she was washing every day. So we didn't have any toys."

That was the way we grew up. We ate stale bread and scraped anything green off the baloney for lunch. Breakfast? Are you kidding. And dinner was what rich kids got.

You know that. You all lived the same way and told your kids the same story. And while your kids were growing up you actually were in the coal mine or up some elevator shaft, either fixing it or riding it to a desk where you spent the entire time that your kids were growing up.

"Daddy, Mommy, did you see how I ran faster than everyone today?"

"Sorry, kid, I was in the coal mine, or up the elevator."

But grandparenthood is different. It is the best. It is not, as many joke, the best when grandkids go away—it is the best when they arrive. For some, most perhaps, the arrival is a long time since the last time and it is from far away.

But honest to heaven there is nothing, totally nothing, better in life than when the kids are coming. The kids of your kids. And we are out of the coal mine and down from the elevator.

It is good to discover one of the best things in life, even if it is in the closing chapters.

"Of course I can catch a ladybug."

"Can you get Joe? Polka Dot Joe?"

"No sweat."

"Come, come Joe, come on ladybug."

I am in the backyard. Ruby, who can make pancakes and French toast and has helped build a dollhouse, is waiting for me to catch Joe.

Easy.

She has a house ready. It is a plastic olive container without the olives and it has grass and flowers inside and holes in the roof. If I were a ladybug I would call it home.

"Here, little ladybug," I said while prowling the yard.

"Here, ladybug."

No ladybug.

"Come on you blankety blank ladybug. Ruby is waiting." I am thinking this, because I would never say "blankety blank" in front of her.

Still no bugs. Usually the complaint is too many mosquitoes, too many flies, too many ... but no, no one has ever complained of too many ladybugs.

Not a ladybug in sight or in hand.

I call some garden shops. Yes, wonderful, I don't believe it. You can actually buy a ladybug.

I figured this was not indulgence, because it would be good to have ladybugs in our backyard—and the neighbour's backyard and their neighbour's backyard. That would get rid of the aphids, which we did not have but we, or our neighbours or their neighbours, might have if we did not have ladybugs.

"Do you have one called Joe?" I ask over the phone of the nice lady in the garden shop.

Silence.

"Do you have a ladybug called Polka Dot Joe?" I repeat.

"No, sir, we have only ladybugs. Ordinary ladybugs."

"No Joe?"

There was a pause. I believe the poor young woman at the other end who wants to spend her life in botany and entomology and selling plants was desperately looking through her catalogue.

Was there a Polka Dot Joe species of ladybug she did not know about?

"I think you should try the university," she said. "They have a more extensive collection."

I thanked her, got the address of the store and told Ruby's mother where it was. This is another advantage of being a grandparent. You shuffle off the jobs of an unbelievably busy parent onto the unbelievably busy parent.

They came back with a bag of ladybugs. You don't get ladybugs in a bag, I thought. You get baloney in a bag. Actually, you get baloney in waxed paper that no one uses anymore and then it is put in a bag.

But not ladybugs. They should come in a jar, or something.

"You are not putting bugs into *my* refrigerator!" said Ruby's grandmother, who did not grow up with bugs in a fridge.

"But that's what the nice lady in the plant store told us to do," said Ruby, who has a way with grandparents.

"But," said grandmother.

"If we don't they will get excited," said Ruby.

"Excited?" said a grandmother staying remarkably calm.

The bag had a plastic window through which we could see a swarm of ladybugs clambering over strips of newspaper. They did not look calm.

"We have to put them in the refrigerator or they will all come out at once when we open the bag and we might not find Polka Dot Joe," said Ruby.

So we cooled down Joe and the ladies until they stopped being so excited and then went outside and opened the bag.

"They're not coming out," said Ruby.

By now her three-year-old sister, Zoe, had come to watch.

"Bugs," said Zoe.

"Yes, ladybugs," said Ruby trying to be an eight-year-old teacher. And then she opened the bag.

"Screech," screamed Zoe when one of the ladybugs came out and flew past her face. Screech again when four or five did the same.

"Close the bag." Ruby or her mother or her grandmother or grandfather said that, or everyone said that at once.

A swarm of hands and fingers tried to stop the great escape.

"Don't hurt them," said Ruby. "You might crush Joe."

The hands loosened, the bag opened, the escape continued.

"Screech," screamed Zoe again as a flock of ladybugs flew at her.

We got the bag closed without killing Joe or anyone else, and then opened it just enough to let out a few at a time.

"A bug," said Zoe.

"No, a lot of bugs," said grandpa, who knows the difference between one and many.

But Zoe was looking at her arm, which had a bug on it.

"A bug," she said again.

"A bug," said grandpa, who is never too old to learn the difference between one and many.

Ruby got four or five into her olive container and closed the lid.

She studied them for a while. "Polka Dot Joe is not in there," she said.

"How do you know?" I asked.

"Well, just look. He's not there," she said.

Her grandmother went through the grass where some of them had fallen and her grandfather was looking in the leaves of a bush. If it was not for this we would have been doing something like laundry or house cleaning or grocery shopping and when the day was over we would have said, "What did we do today? Nothing."

Now we could say we'd been looking for a ladybug, a special ladybug named Joe. You don't get those chances very often.

"Here he is," said Ruby, who was as excited as a warmed-up ladybug.

She got him up from the grass with one finger and put him in the container.

"How do you know that's Polka Dot Joe?" I asked.

"Just look at him. He has polka dots in just the right places."

"But they all have polka dots," I said.

"Not like him."

And that was that. There was no arguing. I have heard that no two ladybugs have the same dots and if I've heard it, it must be so. Besides, Ruby just told me that is Joe, so for sure she/he is Joe.

A short time later they left, with Joe in a jar.

I never had a Polka Dot Joe before in my life. There was no Polka Dot Joe in the coal mine or up in the elevator shaft. Now I had met one, and looked right at his polka dots, I would know a Joe wherever I found one.

And not just that. My neighbours now will have no aphids. Not a bad gift from a grandkid.

Unlikely Love

"Unlikely love?" I said to myself. "I'm not writing about unlikely love."

I had just gotten a note from Harbour Publishing's managing editor, Anna Comfort O'Keeffe, who proposed that title. *Unlikely Love Stories*.

No, I thought. As I said before, I wanted this book to be deep, to be life changing, sort of like those books that sell millions of copies and make you think your life is changing as you read them.

Actually, the only thing I ever read that changed my life was an article in *National Geographic* about Vancouver. It was 1972 and the article said the city was a nice place. One line said the mountains are reflected in the windows of the skyscrapers.

That sounded good. I had never seen a mountain. I asked my wife to read it. She had never seen a mountain. She liked the story. So we moved here. That is basic life changing.

Now the skyscrapers are reflected in the windows of the skyscrapers.

Anyway, I wanted this book to be deep. I don't always write about love stories, I told myself. I write about deep things, I thought, even though I could not think of anything deep.

I had sent Anna a few stories, including the one about Ed and Cathy who work around the old train in the round house. If you haven't read it, please skip ahead. It is touching. Cathy lives in a wheelchair and Ed lives with her. You don't find stuff like this in ordinary life.

But I did not think their love was unlikely. It was beautiful and touching, but when you meet someone you love you know it, you feel it, you become part of two people who want to be one. It is not unlikely. It is the way things should be.

I wrote back and told Anna that I wanted a deeper title, something like *Zen and the Art of Motorcycle Maintenance*, which I never could finish reading because it was so deep, but I loved the title. Then I congratulated Anna for getting married.

For the last book she was Anna Comfort. There was no O'Keeffe in her life.

Congratulations, I wrote to her. Thank you, she said.

"Will he have dinner ready for you when you get home?" I asked when I called about the title.

"No, he would starve if I didn't make him something. He would live on crackers and peanut butter."

Now that is real life. That is real love. That is the kind of comment that keeps people going and keeps them in love and keeps them laughing and happy. It doesn't matter who cooks, so long as each of them knows, and more importantly respects, the value of the other. That is not unlikely.

"So I don't like the title," I said.

"I figured that. Howard told me you would want to change it. You always want to change it."

Howard is Howard White, the publisher of Harbour Publishing. When I say publisher I am speaking about, in my world, the true story god. Publishers hold all power. Publishers say "Yes" or "No" to a manuscript that someone has worked on for their entire lives, or at least since they took a creative writing course.

If you are a writer, publishers are *always* right.

And he is right this time—I *would* like something else. But I don't know what else, just something else.

Then today, May 13, 2012, Mother's Day, I am with cameraman Al Coen looking for a moment that would make Mother's Day extra special. I have no idea what that is, but I am looking for it, which is not easy when you don't know what you are looking for.

We go into a park and see a large group of Filipinos having a picnic.

"No," I say, "no story, Filipinos get together for any reason. They love the family."

They are good, they are wonderful, but I want something unusual and this is not it.

Way over there is another large group. Same thing. Filipinos. If you want to see folks who have fun together, get invited to a Filipino party.

But wait. Look over there, between the two big parties. There are two people sitting alone. That is beautiful. I have no idea why it is beautiful, but in their small isolation between the large families they look touching. Can you sit in a park on Mother's Day without children? Of course.

If they had no children, that can be touching. If they had children and they are not here, that can be touching. Everything works, it just depends on whether you let it.

We say hello and ask if we can take a picture of them because they look so different from the big parties nearby. Then I ask gingerly if they are together. You never know. They might be old friends, or new friends.

"We have been married thirty years," said the woman. "We met one day and got married the next."

Before I can say, "Are you kidding?" she adds, "No one believes us, but it is true."

The heck with a Mother's Day story, this is golden.

"But we had only one rule," said the man, whose name is Gregory. "If we did not understand each other we would get a divorce."

He laughed. "I've been waiting thirty years to understand."

Bingo, something hit the inside of my head. A thought. This is very unlikely.

"He said he wanted a thin woman," she said. Her name is Helen and she was patting her full and comfortable-looking stomach. "I said you will have to wait a while."

"I am still waiting," he laughed.

In less than one minute of conversation it was clear that when you laugh at what you don't have, or wish you had or didn't have, none of that remains a problem

"Children?" I asked.

"Only his daughter," Helen said. "Everyone told me 'Don't do it, don't become a stepmother, don't take on the responsibility,' but I did."

She was a teenager at the time.

"And does she live here?"

"Live here? She should *be* here!"

Then Helen's cell phone rang.

"Where are you?"

Pause.

"Look for the two large families. We are the little family between them."

She stood up looking for the girl she had raised. Mother's Day was happening in front of us.

The daughter and her husband and their sixteen-month-old son were coming. Helen was running to meet them. She picked up and hugged her grandson.

"Now it is Mother's Day," she said

"She is the best mother in the world, and the best grandmother," said the girl who had become a woman whom Helen had been warned not to let into her family.

They went off together and Al, the cameraman, who was capturing the scene, suddenly turned to me and said, "My eyes are wet. I don't believe this, my eyes are wet."

News cameramen see many things without their eyes getting wet.

And then the little boy ran off in the grass and grandma chased after him and the daughter, who was now a mother, was kissed by her husband, who arrived pushing a stroller full of the stuff of picnics. And, still sitting in his chair, the man who asked a woman to marry him after knowing her only one day, smiled.

As it turns out, the title of this book is perfect, because there is no better way to describe what love is than unlikely. I wish I could think of something like that. Thanks, Anna.

P.S. As we were leaving the park I saw a fellow practising casting with a fly rod in a big, empty grassy area. His arm went back behind his head while he was holding the rod and then waved it forward and back again, like wheat bending slowly in a breeze.

(Actually, I have never seen wheat bending in a breeze. The few times I have been near a wheat field, it is so packed that it would take a tornado to bend it, but the gently waving wheat is still a nice image.)

He moved the rod back and forth, with the long, silky fishing line coming out at the tip floating in the air. That is an image you may have seen in some television commercial. It is gentle and beautiful.

If there is any weight at the end it is no more than a fly, which is no weight at all and why it is called fly-fishing.

Probably the fisherman was practising so that he could go fishing and get the fly to land where he wanted on the water. But anyone who has ever done that, or even watched it being done, knows that the fish is the dessert. The fishing is the main course.

The movement, the swaying, the watching, the floating, that is the art that takes over the mind and catches the peace that releases the problems.

I once talked to another man casting with a fly rod on a grassy spot in the crowded West End. There was no hook, no weight, no danger. He cast in the classic way, one arm waving the rod and the other playing out the line further and further. He said he had back problems, neck problems, head problems and just plain problems until he started doing this.

He never got his line wet. He never went fishing. On the other hand, he lost all his problems.

Anything you do peacefully that you like to do—tai chi, basketball, gardening, meditation, fly-fishing—is the perfect thing to do, for you. It releases your mind from everything and somehow puts you in a space of peace. It is not mystic philosophy. It just works. No fooling. Try it. Do something you like and you will forget the things you don't like.

But the picture of the man with the fly rod belongs here, after a love story, because it reminded me of one thing I saw a long time ago.

Two men were practising casting with a fly rod on a patch of dry land. One, the younger man, had his arms around the frail older man.

"Let it go back and forth, now back again, and again. Now let the line out," said the younger man.

The older man followed his instructions and the plastic filament floated on the air like a butterfly catching a breeze.

"Beautiful," said the younger man.

I waited until he had reeled the line back in and then I interrupted. You don't cut in when a fishing line is in the air. It's not like cutting in on a dance while the music is on and a couple is together. You can get away with that so long as you are bigger than the man doing the dancing and the woman really wants to dance with you. Otherwise you are risking your life.

But interrupting in the middle of a fly rod casting can have a much bigger consequence. You may kill a perfect moment, and that can never be replayed.

"Excuse me," I said, softly.

As it turned out the younger man was the son of the older man who was being held in his son's arms.

"He taught me to cast when I was a kid," said the younger man. "Now he has Alzheimer's and he has forgotten, so I am teaching him again."

It is close to never that I have heard such beautiful words. So much kindness, so much patience. So much giving up so that someone else could relive a moment of beauty. So much love.

That is why this small postscript follows a love story. It is not about fishing. It is about holding your love with a fishing line, unlikely as that may be.

Erik and Ole

You have met them before, but this is real life, and things happen in real life.

I was working with Roger Hope, a cameraman, and he wanted to know more of the history of the only black community that ever was in Vancouver. I had told him that the city decided to put in a freeway that went right through the community and destroyed it.

But it was not much of a freeway. It was a half-kilometre of freeway that started at one end of the black area and ended at the other. Then the freeway stopped and construction stopped and the blacks were gone. This is where Jimmy Hendrix's grandmother lived.

That story was in the last book and I had already told him about it.

"Let me show you something neat, a house that was beachfront property in 1910 but now has a road in front of it and a park and another road and railroad tracks."

This was also in the last book, but I have to keep you up to date. In fact, I have to keep myself moving with the times by revisiting the old times and old places.

We pulled up to the house and I said, "What the . . . heck?"

It was boarded up. The windows and the front door had plywood covering them. A For Sale sign hung in front.

"He must be dead," I said to Roger.

"Who?"

"One of the neatest guys. And I missed it."

I was not happy.

I called the real estate agent listed on the sign. Yes, Erik had passed away and the house was for sale. In fact, it was sold yesterday and the agent was coming back today to hang the Sold sign on it.

"Who sold it?"

"A friend of Erik's."

Oh, my lord. Really? The last time I was here Erik had only one friend, Ole. And Ole and Erik had been in an argument about the value of a pickup truck that Ole had sold to Erik.

"It's no good, it doesn't run," said Erik with a Danish accent.

"It was running fine until you got it," said Ole with the same accent.

They had been arguing for sixty years. They argued about the Canucks and about the government and about the weather.

"If we didn't argue there would be nothing for us to talk about," said Ole.

"It's always you who starts the arguments," said Erik.

They met on a ship coming to Canada. They moved to Vancouver together. They drank beer together. They waited for each other to call and visit.

"He is the cause of all my problems," said Erik.

"He would not know how to live without me," said Ole.

Erik's hands were huge and powerful and calloused, and the

crevices that once were wrinkles were almost deep enough to put a child's fingers into.

Ole's forearms were made of muscles that looked like coils of wire. Both men were welders.

When Erik's house was built in 1910 it was next to False Creek. There was a stream that had salmon in it that ran near the front. Times change things. Cars were now parked in front of the house and condos were on each side.

"I would never sell," said Erik. "Why should I? This is my home and what would I do with the money? Nothing. I will die in here."

And then he did.

But he left the house to Ole, who got $800,000 for it. Erik paid $6,000 in 1957. He had no family. He never married. Ole was his family. But on this day Ole was in the hospital having a hernia operation. I could not talk with him.

I knew, or rather I guessed, but it was a good guess, that Ole would leave the money to his children and his grandchildren, and that the lives of some kids would change forever.

That is the way things happen in life, in real life. Even in death, the endings are not always bad.

More Unlikely

March 3, 2012

On this day I saw in the newspaper that it was the twenty-first anniversary of Rodney King getting beaten by the Los Angeles police.

There are some of you too young to remember that, but you should know about it. It was a case that once again reshaped America, and therefore much of the world and how it thinks.

A black guy was stopped after racing a car at more than 100 miles per hour in the city. It was not an easy stop. You do not stop cars going that fast without a lot of other cars and sirens and adrenalin. And when they did get him stopped he would not get out of his car. He put up a fight and many police responded, and they hit him with night sticks and kicked him and it was an ugly scene.

The one thing about it was, it was videotaped. Someone watching said they would use their new camera and record this. And then he sent the tape to a television station. And overnight it became the world's biggest story.

To most, like me, it was another beating of another black man. That hurt. That is one of the reasons I left America.

There were mitigating circumstances, as they say in court when they have a look at the crime after everyone is cleaned up and dressed up in a suit and has had a haircut. The mitigating circumstance was that Rodney King was high on cocaine and in that state the culprit often displays superhuman strength and defiance.

He feels no pain. He has no fear. He fights beyond human belief.

And so the police do the same. And it is ugly.

Except it was in the camera and the next day it was everywhere, and I was so angry, so disappointed that nothing had changed in my country since I had left it. I went into my backyard and began digging.

I was furious. I was mad. I grabbed a shovel and dug. Never before in my life had I had a backyard and now that I had one in a country separated from my native country I felt free, but angry.

I had no point in my digging. It was just that it was taking the anger out of me. I dug until it got dark and then kept digging. I dug until my waist was even with the ground. I dug until I had a problem getting out of the hole. But I felt better.

What happened after that was that a friend told me how I could turn the hole into a fish pond, and for the next ten years I had some peace and some war in my backyard.

The fish pond was beautiful, but the raccoons ate the fish. So I put chicken wire around the pond. The raccoons climbed over the wire. I put chicken wire over the top. The raccoons went under the wire. So I staked it. They reached through it and rolled the stones I had inside into the pond.

So I put up a double wall of wire. (I have written about this before, so if you know the story just skip to a little later and it will get updated.) The raccoons ripped apart the wire. So I put plywood between the rows of steel webbing. And plywood on top.

I beat them. But now I couldn't see the fish.

There is a lesson in life in that. Sometimes, when the fight is too big or the mountain too high, you either lose or pick a smaller mountain. I filled in the pond and planted zucchini. They were delicious.

And then it was the anniversary of the beating of Rodney King and I wanted to write the story of the fish pond but there was nothing new in it.

I have read a good deal about Rodney King. In short, he was a drug addict and an alcoholic, and he was in trouble and in jail more than most ordinary folks. He did nothing with his life either before or after the incident that affected so many people.

There was nothing to write about.

There is a note for myself in the first manuscript of this book: "Rodney King," it says. "Write something uplifting." There was nothing written after it.

Then came June 18, 2012. Early in the morning, when I read the computer version of the newspaper, I saw that Rodney King, at forty-seven, had died the day before. He drowned in a swimming pool. I had still learned nothing from him.

On that same day I saw a woman in Queen Elizabeth Park who was both blind and lost. I knew she was lost because she had stopped walking and was swinging her white cane back and forth on the sidewalk, and her face seemed perplexed.

"Can I help you?" I asked.

She was looking for one street but was walking toward another street.

"It is that way," I said. Then I realized that is stupid. "It is in the opposite direction to the way you are walking," I said again, this time thinking.

"Thank you," she said.

And then I remembered, she was the same woman about whom I wrote several books ago, when we saw her stuck behind a wooden barricade on a street that was getting ripped up. The construction workers had gone home and she was alone on a dirt road having no idea which way to go and no feeling with the tip of her white cane.

I helped her back to Main Street. I wrote about that because it was in praise of the cameraman who saw her and drove back to rescue her. I did the guiding, but it was Tony Clark, the same fellow in the *Getting to the Bubble* book, who saw her lost.

Same woman, different location.

"I go for a walk every day, for about an hour or an hour and a half," she said.

Then she said the most amazing thing.

"I go different places every few days."

How the heck in the world does a blind woman go for a walk in different places?

"I manage," she said. "Sometimes I get lost, but if I call for help someone will help me."

We talked. She had been blind for thirty-six years. She was born with an ailment that she could not pronounce. She had had bad sight as a child. She could not read the blackboard in school, so they thought she was not smart and they put her in the back of the class.

And then one day as an adult, when she was in a supermarket, her sight just went.

"I could see nothing. I could still see a little when I went in, but suddenly everything went away. It was scary."

I'll say. Scary? That is hardly the word. She went blind in the aisles of soup cans. She felt her way out of the store and has never seen anything since then.

She met a man at the Canadian Institute for the Blind and they married thirty-five years ago.

"And we are still married." She laughed.

He was partly blind, but in bending over to pick up something he accidentally hit something sticking out of a work bench and it poked his good eye. That was three months ago, she told me. From that moment on he was, like her, totally blind.

"Does he go walking with you?" I asked.

She laughed. "No, he can't keep up. But that is because he just went blind. He is not used to it."

We walked together for a while. I knew enough to offer her my arm and not take hers. I asked questions. She talked.

"What I wish for most is that people would talk to me," she said. "I can hear them right around me, but they say nothing, not even excuse me. I wish someone would say 'Hello' or something."

Bing, like a bell. She sounded like Cathy in the wheelchair in the story the *Love Train Again*, who said what she wished for was someone to touch her.

So sad. So easy to fix.

And then we got to the street she was heading for. Every day she goes for a walk, every day she has the courage to try something new and take on the world even though she is only five foot one and a little bent over.

She said she knew where she was going and thanked me. And then she was gone.

This was the same day I read that Rodney King had died. His beating and his story set off riots, and made me dig a hole.

Joan did nothing but take a walk.

When I got home I saw my note about Rodney King. I had nothing to say about him. He did not change my life. Joan did.

June 18 a year from now it will be the anniversary of the day I walked with Joan. She is worth remembering.

The Magic of That Old Horse

was sneezing. I had hay fever. I still have hay fever. If you have hay fever and it is spring and your eyes are driving you crazy with itching and you are sneezing and the tissue paper in your hand is dripping and can't hold any more bodily fluids, you know about hay fever.

If you don't have hay fever I don't want to talk to you. You don't know. You are blessed and we who suffer hate you.

Actually, I am sneezing so much I don't have the energy to hate, or open my eyes or stand up.

The phone rings. It is my buddy Dave McKay, the barbecue king and cameraman.

"I have a great story for you."

Ahhh-choo. "I don't want it. I just want to blow . . ." haa-choo "my nose."

"It's about a horse."

Good heavens, no. Please, no. Not a horse. Not any animal. I did not grow up with animals or plants, so when I meet animals or plants I sneeze.

So I said to Dave, "Nooo. Not a horse. Anything but a horse. They make me sneeze."

"It's an old horse."

That is a weakness. I like old things, people, horses, cars. I also like children and ponies and once every ten years I like a new car.

He tells me that the police department has just gotten two new horses and he was taking pictures of them for the news and one of the members of the mounted squad told him there is an old man of a horse and he is cranky.

Even with a runny nose, who could resist a cranky old horse?

We go to the stable in Stanley Park and I have got to tell you the police horses have it good. Their stalls are the size of some Yaletown condos, the more expensive ones. And right in the middle of a row of condo stalls is Piko.

He is eating.

"He gets softened alfalfa cubes," said Constable Conrad Van Dyke. "His teeth are a little weak and these are easy to chew."

Three times a day the cubes are soaked in water before he gets them. This is a special horse.

Then the good constable walks Piko out of the covered stable and I watch as the tips of the toes of his hind hoofs drag on the floor. He is an old man shuffling down the hallway.

Outside he gets a long walk in a big circle, like a dog on a leash, except he is going slowly and he is not being encouraged to go any faster.

Two other horses with riders, both women with guns, come back from patrol. You do not have to get romantic or fictional to see that Piko is watching them. It is more than just curiosity. He is studying both of the horses, who are new on the force.

"He watches every one of them," said Sergeant Doug McMillan.

"He was the alpha male while he was here and he still thinks he is. On his very first day back he snapped at a horse who was in his old stall.

The story: He had been on the force for ten years. He had faced large crowds, he had been petted by little kids. He learned the almost impossible lesson of not rearing up at the crack of a firing pistol. And when he was twenty-five, retirement age, he was given to a therapeutic riding organization.

For the next five years he carried children with nightmares in their day times. The children with unimaginable pains and uncontrollable muscles were rocked slowly and carefully while sitting on his saddle. For some strange reason, almost every kid in need gets some of those needs answered on the back of a slow and gently moving horse.

"One day his hindquarters gave out. He was carrying a child, but no one was hurt," said the sergeant who was stroking Piko's face.

The therapeutic centre called the police stables. What should they do?

There was only one answer. The police were not going to abandon an old friend. In only the time it took to get a trailer hooked up, they drove to the centre.

"We brought Piko home," said the sergeant.

That was a while ago. He is in retirement back home. As he was led back to his stall, I watched as he walked down the aisle between two rows of stalls. The other horses looked over their gates. One got up from a sleep to watch Piko walk by. It was uncanny. It was eerie.

Later the fellow who writes the introductions of the stories for the news, Tim Perry, said, "I could not believe that. The other horses watched him. One even got up. That was probably the magic moment of the entire show."

Tim Perry has seen thousands, no, tens of thousands, of stories. He rarely comments. He just writes what he sees and others read it. But this time he said it was "magical." I have seldom felt so good.

Piko is thirty years old. Horses like him usually live about thirty years.

And here he is in his own stall, and coming down the aisle in the stable is Constable Susan Sharp, with a gun in a holster and a steaming bucket in her hand.

"Piko's tea," said Susan. She is part of the new force that fits in with a younger society that has women in charge of many, if not most, things. She is pretty. Not the big, tough cop. She is young. Not the old guy with wrinkles. She carries a gun. Okay, she does have an old-fashioned job to do.

She put down the heated water and opened the gate to Piko's stall.

"Do the other horses get hot water?" I asked. I knew the answer, but when it was spoken it made Piko sound more special.

"Only Piko," she said.

And Dave took a picture of Piko drinking his steaming tea. He was the old man in his golden years being catered to by a loving staff of caregivers. It is good when a story and a life have a good ending.

This is nice, but not profound. It is a sweet story, but not life changing. It has little effect outside of those who care for the horse feeling good and the horse feeling good.

At least that is what I thought as we left the horses' compound and walked back to Dave's truck. Then my eyes started itching and I started sneezing.

Oh, my heavens. A most severe allergy to horses and hay had disappeared while I was next to a horse and standing in a stable full of hay.

Is that possible?

Is it possible that simply learning that something good was happening had changed the chemistry in my body?

I don't know if this goes to the degree of practitioners of some Eastern philosophies who say they can operate on patients without anaesthetic. They say they can do this if the patients believe they will feel no pain and then there is no pain.

I am not going to try that.

But I do know that for an unbelievable twenty minutes I was with a horse and I was not itching or sneezing. I also know that I was transfixed by the story of the horse. There was no thought of myself or my problems or my sneezing while I listened to the story of Piko and watched him drinking his afternoon tea.

What I know for a fact is that if you are interested in someone or something other than yourself your problems go away.

Pretty good lesson from an old horse. And now that I am thinking about myself I will sneeze right through the night.

Back on the Love Train

All I did was kiss her, and it was only on the cheek. I had no idea what that meant. I had no idea how wonderful and sad and beautiful and desperate a kiss on the cheek could be.

In the last book, *Here's Mike*, I told you the love story of Cathy and Ed. They were the volunteer hosts in the old Roundhouse that holds the steam engine with the numbers 374.

Once upon a time that ancient hunk of black steel on wheels was very important. It was the first engine to cross the country and it pulled the first line of cars with passengers from Toronto and Montreal who ended up in Vancouver.

It was an unbelievable journey, almost like the first rocket to the moon. How could an engine burning wood have the strength to cross the Rockies and then get through and over the mountains and rivers of British Columbia? Unbelievable, but it happened. And because it did, British Columbia remained part of Canada.

If it had not been for that train pulled by that engine, the good citizens of Vancouver and distant surrounding lands would have voted to join the United States.

That is interesting, except in truth most people see it, touch it, climb up to where the engineer drove and the fireman threw the hunks of wood into the fire, climb down and say, "Un huh. Can we have lunch now?"

History is fascinating if you want it to be. Otherwise it is just something that happened back then and it cannot compete against a hamburger.

But love, now that is entirely different. When you see a couple hugging it feels good, even if you are just watching. But don't watch too long or you may get jealous, which is normal, and you may have feelings inside yourself that could be embarrassing. Love is not a slouch of an emotion.

We went to see the old engine but when we got there we were taken up with Ed touching Cathy's hair. Love, when it comes to people who don't fit the image of young lovers or beautiful people, can hold your attention. Love with well-made bodies and soft faces and flowing hair is what you expect to see. They are the ones who make you jealous because you are none of the above.

But when you see love in a wheelchair, love with a long white beard, love with no ability to stand, love with years packed high and deep, then you get to see the stuff that puts love as the number one emotion for life.

Instead of using all those words, just imagine the picture. Ed looked like Santa Claus playing with Cathy's hair. Cathy was wrapped in a blanket, her face was twitching. Her head jerked to the side, then back again. She has cerebral palsy, a curse you are born with and die with. There is no time off for good behaviour.

Neither one had a well-made body or a soft face. And that is what makes love so profoundly incredible. In the last book, I talked about how they met and grew closer. He is a widower. She had never been married, or had a boyfriend, or been on a date, or danced, or gone anywhere with any male other than a paid caregiver.

By the time I met them they were living together, exploring the city together and going to movies together. That was better than the old steel steam engine. Love beats steam engines any day.

Sometime later she wrote to me on the computer. I don't know how that is done. I think computers are wonderful. My quadriplegic niece writes to me. She can't move her fingers, but she writes. That is amazing.

Cathy asked if I would visit her and Ed at the Roundhouse and sign her book.

She looked the same. He looked the same. I shook his hand. I hugged Cathy and kissed her on the cheek. We were no longer strangers. I had written about her. That makes us old friends.

She later wrote back and said the kiss was the best part of her day. That was nice.

Her story grew incredibly after that. She thought she was an only child. She had had a twin brother, but he died shortly after birth, so she never knew him. She did know that she was put into the government's care when she was a baby. She knew she grew up in institutions with little or no care. She knew she was left alone for hours, sometimes days, in empty rooms at the end of empty hallways. She could not complain, she could not move. She could only cry.

She lived like that for much of her life until she met Ed and, however that happened, her life started.

And then, about six months after I met her, she got a call from her sister. She did not know she had a sister. This was very exciting.

One of her sisters (yes, one of them, because there were more) called her. Thora had been hunting for her family. She did not know if she had a family, but she knew she was adopted at birth and had been taken in by a wonderful family, and until now she had felt that looking for her natural family might betray them.

She was wrong. Most of those who adopt kids are loving and strong enough to understand that the child they have raised might someday want to find another family. That does not mean the child does not love their adopted parents.

Thora went hunting, and found Cathy. And then Barb was found. All three were living a short car ride away from each other. Okay, a short car ride and a ferry ride, and adding the price of ferry rides is enough to stifle the hunt for a sister, but they persisted and in the end there were hugs and tears.

And then another sister was found in California, and then another was found in Alberta—five sisters who had never seen each other. For a pair of alcoholic parents who could not face bringing up kids, they were very productive.

That is a beautiful story. But it is not the story that turned my heart and told me about the meaning of a kiss.

Cathy gave me some things she had written. She hoped to get them published and since I have a publisher who puts my words into books she thought maybe I could help her.

Her writing is little more than twenty pages. It is about her childhood in institutions where she was left alone for hours, actually for days and weeks and months and years. It is about being yelled at and cursed by caregivers. Imagine being yelled at when you cannot move an arm or a leg. It is about wanting to kill herself, if only she could.

At the end of her writing is the warmth of meeting Ed, who was kind to her and talked to her and made her feel like life was worth living.

That is all beautiful.

But there is one thing she wrote that taught me we are such fools and have so much to learn.

It was a few pages with the title: *Touch: It's a Good Thing.*

She begins: "Without touch you can die."

I read that, then reread it. And I thought of a time when I was small, after my mother had left my father and I was alone much of the time. There was one night when my mother had a few friends and relatives for a party.

I was in bed in a dark room at the back of a hallway and could hear them laughing and clinking glasses and lighting cigarettes with Zippo lighters. And then the door opened and my aunt, my mother's sister, came into the room and put her hand on my head and said good night to me.

Sixty years later I remember that moment and the feel of her hand. It was so good. I felt something, probably love and security and comfort, but I had none of those words. I just felt something and I went to sleep. I still thank her for that.

Cathy said: "I feel that many people still have a problem touching individuals who are disabled. The reasons for these problems are many. Part of it might be ignorance, but mostly I think it is fear, fear that they may hurt me in some way, fear that my disability is somehow contagious, fear that they may get into trouble with me or someone else if they 'invade my personal space.' These fears are often exacerbated by my electric wheelchair. I wish people (this included, in the past, staff people) could get over this, because it was contact with others that finally helped me to start healing."

I thought of something else. This will sound like it is self-praise, but it is just something I did one day and someone commented on it and I thought the comment was so, so ... what? So complimentary to me, but it should not have been anything out of the ordinary.

In the 1980s there were no homeless people in Vancouver. There were just some drunks who slept under the Georgia Viaduct, mostly because steam pipes kept it warm and the roadway above kept it dry and no one would bother them there.

And then we got reports of a woman living off to the side of the

Mary Hill Bypass. That is a road entering Vancouver. It was remote back then. The woman lived under a tarp over some shopping carts and people would throw wrapped-up sandwiches and fruit to her.

I went out to talk. I lifted the tarp and said, "Hello." She said, quote, "Get the hell out of here."

The loving warmth of a homeless person.

Time passed. I did numerous stories about the Mary Hill Bypass Woman. (See? Everyone and everything gets a name.) Then, after enough stories, the government took an interest and she was arrested (that is a terrible word) under the Mental Health Act and taken to Royal Columbian Hospital, where she was given a bath and psychological testing. They go together like cheese and a rat trap.

You do not have to put homeless people through batteries of government-funded tests. You only have to help them get a place to live. If they don't want it, you have to accept that and wish them good luck.

The Mary Hill Bypass Woman passed the mental tests of the government and was released from the hospital and went back to her shopping carts and her home with no roof or walls. She moved from the bypass to a park in the next town, Coquitlam, and then to Stanley Park, the city's jewel, not a home for the homeless. I did a story about her living on the banks of Lost Lagoon.

By this time she had gotten to recognize me.

"You again?" she would say at our meetings. And by now I had learned her name. Linda Black.

"Yes, me again. Ladies who live under shopping carts are not very common," I would say. "How come you came here, to Stanley Park?" I asked.

"Why not? It's pretty here. Everyone wants to come here."

You cannot argue with that. She was not crazy, she just wanted to be near Lost Lagoon, where most everyone in Vancouver wants to be. Except she did not want a condo. She was happy with her cart.

She disappeared again, and then reappeared like a thought you lose and then regain in the middle of a conversation. I never knew when she would be gone or when or where she would come back.

She came back near the First Avenue exit of Highway One. Someone called me. He said she had set up camp just at the exit and he was worried that if someone came off the highway too fast and too drunk she might be run over. I should do something, he said.

I went for a visit to Linda. There was a cameraman with me. I am lucky. Things I don't expect to happen end up on television.

She crawled out of her hovel of canned food and bedding and paperback books under a tarp that was draped over her shopping cart and said "Hello." We were almost friends.

I told her someone was worried that she might be killed if she stayed here and she might consider moving around the corner.

"Killed?" she said. "What's wrong with that?"

I had no answer. I stepped forward, put my arms out and she moved into them and I hugged her, and then kissed her, on the cheek (I am not going to let my wife think I get closer than just a cheek), and then I squeezed her again.

"That feels good," she said to me.

And then we parted. I never saw her again. I know she moved the next day because her cart was gone. I heard that she went to Burnaby, and then that she'd been seen down by the Fraser River. It doesn't matter where her last home was. It was just another place. What does matter is that she was gone, and she died without a home. Her body was scraped up by the coroner, who had been told by sanitation workers who sometimes have the sadness of finding discards, on the sidewalks or in alleys, that no one should have to discover, because they should not be there in the first place.

Her body would have been stored in the morgue for a few months and then sent to the Fraserview crematorium. That is where all the homeless end up. They are turned into ashes and dust, and each is stored and labelled in a small cardboard box along with stacks of others who had no one to say they knew them.

Eventually a hole would be dug with a backhoe in the grounds of the cemetery and fifty or one hundred boxes of ashes of former human beings would be carefully placed inside. Then the dirt would be shovelled back in and, except for a record that consisted of a number instead of a name, they would be completely gone.

That was Linda Black. Except that after I did the story about her living by the highway exit, a woman friend of mine, Ruth Olde, mother of six, called me. It had to be a woman.

"I saw you kiss that woman," she said. "Not many would. That must have made her feel good."

That was the best compliment I ever got on any story.

And in no way do I mean this as self-flattery. The compliment was to the kiss. The touch. The feel and the hug and the pressing of one body to another. I felt good and I believe Linda felt good.

When I read Cathy's words I thought of Linda. And I thought of my aunt touching my head. It is so easy to change the world, at least of one person. It is so easy to make things better.

Just touch someone.

And I cannot leave it there. Have you ever seen the painting on the ceiling of the Sistine Chapel? This has nothing to do with religion. I don't care what you believe or don't believe, but one of the greatest artists of all time, Michelangelo, painted the birth of everything up there.

Everything does not just start with God, but with his index finger just finishing a touch with Adam, who held out his finger. You have seen the picture. It is so famous that the entire ceiling is often reduced to two fingertips, almost touching, just separating after coming together. It is beautiful. This stuff about touching is nothing new.

And Michelangelo, as you probably know, was a physically twisted, ugly fellow with few friends and even fewer who would touch him.

He knew what made it all work.
So does Cathy.
So did Linda.
So did my aunt.
And you do, too.

The Window and the Weirdo

How could this happen? The chance of it is less than a winning lottery ticket.

In 1973 a fellow who was twenty and had a newborn son was living above a corner store. It was the only apartment he could afford.

He looked out the window and saw a couple of kids below leaving the store. One of them, a little girl, had a bag of sweets.

"Hey," the fellow in the window shouted down, "Can I have some of your candy?" Smart-aleck comment.

The little girl with the candy was frightened. Of course she was. A weirdo up above was talking to her.

"Let's get out of here, that fellow is strange," she said to her brother, who had his own candy.

Brother glanced up, she did not. They ran home to grandma's house and ate their candy. It was a passing experience, never mentioned again.

Little girl, who was ten years old at the time, grew up, got married, moved away, had children, got divorced.

Weirdo upstairs got older, lost his hair, got divorced.

He is Gary. She is Diane.

Time passes, as it has done since the beginning, whenever that was.

Gary was in a pub in Fernie. Diane was in a pub in Fernie. This is very far from the east side of Vancouver.

A friend of a friend says to Diane that the guy playing pool is not so bad and if she would like to meet this friend she could introduce her to him.

Diane says No. She has had it with men.

"Oh, come on. He won't bite," says the friend.

After a few more refusals Diane agrees, just to quiet the friend.

They play. He wins. They part. He calls. She says no, no date. No dinner. No drinks.

He calls again. And again.

She gives in. Just to get rid of him.

They eat. They talk. They are both from Vancouver. Imagine that. They are both from the east side. Really?

They both lived in the same neighbourhood. Can't be.

There was a corner store.

Yes, remember that.

Me too, I lived above it.

No. It can't be. Did you ever look out the window and say . . .

Are you kidding? Are you the little girl who had the candy?

No. I mean yes.

Time passed, again.

How did that happen? No one knows. But it did.

Not right away (get real, he was weird back then), not right away, but eventually, they moved in together. The ten-year difference disappears when you are in your forties and beyond.

Eventually: Will you marry me?

Yes.

And twenty-five years after that pool game that's where I met them, outside the corner store. They could not believe it was still there. And the window was still there. They looked up, holding hands. He let go and put his arm around her shoulders. She moved closer.

"I can't believe it," he said.

What was it he could not believe? The window? The coincidence? The fact that they have been married for a long time and are more in love than when they first fell in love?

"I can't believe it, either," said Diane.

She meant all of the above.

How did it happen? I am not going to give you an answer. I don't have one. But it happened. And things like this do happen. That is all that matters.

Anvil Battery, Again, with a Bigger Bang

I don't know how I missed them before. I go to the Hyack Anvil Battery celebrations almost every year, and yet I did not see them.

Someone, something, was probably saving them up for today.

It was raining—no, it was pouring—on the celebration of Queen Victoria's birthday in New Westminster. This should not happen, because there are few other places as loyal to the memory of their Queen than New West.

I have told you before how the good citizens of New West fired a twenty-one-gun salute to their Queen back in the early 1860s when New Westminster was the capital of British Columbia. They felt especially close to the Queen, whose stern face and eyes hung on almost every wall. Not only was she their Queen, but she personally had named their city.

It was originally called Queensborough by the captain of the Royal Engineers who settled the site, but the Queen did not like the name and changed it to New Westminster after the section of London that was, and still is, home to the English parliament. A very important name for a very important place, she said.

New West was now the capital of the new colony of British Columbia and the folks living there were delighted. On their Queen's next birthday they fired the only cannon they had twenty-one times in her honour.

But then the story got dirty and nasty and vindictive because politics and human nature entered.

The governor of the colony did not like New Westminster. That was James Douglas, a giant of a man who rose up from running a Hudson's Bay outpost in Victoria to the top of politics, the governor of a colony.

To his credit he saved the West Coast from being taken over by America. In the late 1850s there were about 40,000 Americans in the Lower Mainland compared to less than one hundred Brits. The Americans were heading up the Fraser looking for gold. They brought with them guns and whiskey and gold pans and the US flag. It was flying at campsites from Hope to Boston Bar. You now know where that name came from.

Mr. Douglas wrote to his Queen and said do something or you will not have anything left to do anything with. She proclaimed the entire area a British Colony. I have written about this before so you know all about it. But it is still amazing to think that if the ship with the proclamation had run aground somewhere off the coast of South America or had sunk or got stuck in the doldrums, the paper with the royal seal would not have arrived before the Americans said, "Hey, we like this place. Let's stay and put Old Glory up on the flag pole."

It could have happened.

But Douglas got to read the Queen's order and where you are now sitting became part of the British empire.

However, Governor Douglas did not like New West. That was

all there was to it. It was filled with Americans and it had too many saloons and it was loud and dirty and, well, that is enough. When you don't like a place there is nothing good you can say about it.

This is part of the story that I have not written about, but a little dirt is always good in the news.

Douglas liked Victoria, where he had run his store and where the ladies dressed as Englishwomen would and where some of the streets were starting to get wooden boards over the mud. Victoria was home, and when you like a place there is nothing bad you can say about it.

When Vancouver Island was included in the colony about seven years later, Douglas arbitrarily said to New West, "You are no longer the capital. Victoria is." That is all there was to it, except for the little detail of a vote in the House of Assembly.

There were two speeches scheduled, one for and one against moving the capital. The speech for moving was read and it stated the position that it was good, for various reasons, none of which made any real sense, given that Victoria was way over there and most of the colony was way over here.

Then William Franklyn, who wanted the capital to stay in New West, got up to read his speech.

"What is this?" he thought as he looked through his papers. This was not the beginning of what he was going to say. He looked some more. He started to read the first paragraph on the first page that was looking up at him. He had written it, but it made no sense. So he read it again, hoping the second time it would make sense. And he read it again.

The assembly groaned and laughed and stomped their boots.

The shyster in the plot was another member of the assembly, William Cox, who was in favour of moving the capital. He had slipped into the room before Franklyn's speech and shuffled the pages. As was the practice in that time, the pages were not numbered.

Then, when Franklyn was red faced and desperately trying to get his pages in order, Cox said, "Let me help."

But what he did was get hold of Franklyn's eye glasses and, whoops. "Oh, I am so sorry. I seem to have knocked the glass right out."

Poor Franklyn, who was pro New West, could see nothing. The assembly recessed while he got his glasses patched up and his speech back in order, but then the Speaker of the Assembly, John Sebastian Helmcken, refused to give Franklyn a second chance to speak. It just so happened that Helmcken was from Victoria.

The vote was 13 to 8 in favour of moving the capital to the tiny town at the bottom of an island a full day's sail away from most of the colony, and James Douglas was happy.

This made great newspaper stories, just as similar things do now, making us shake our heads and say, "What? We elected these people?"

One of the first things the new government in Victoria did was forbid any other city from officially celebrating the Queen's birthday. That would be the singular right of the new capital. They even took away the cannon from New West just to make sure.

The rest of the story you know. The people of New West were angry, but they didn't let it go at that. They got even. The mayor was a blacksmith, and on the Queen's birthday, right in the middle of town, he set up an anvil, put gun powder on top, put another anvil on top of that, and a long pole with a red-hot tip did the trick. Boom, twenty-one times.

Since that day, every Victoria Day except one has been celebrated with the ear-shattering and, in the last decade, car-alarm-activating explosions of twenty-one anvil salutes. The only time there was silence was in 1901 when Queen Victoria died.

Anyway, as I was saying, I don't know how I missed them in all the years I have been to the celebrations in New Westminster.

It was obviously a sweet and touching story but, as in all newspaper,

TV and radio news, the bad news comes first. First the headlines of corruption and sneaky politics, and then we get the nice stories, usually not until the end of the hour and then only if there is room.

The rain was pounding in the parking lot and on the seats in the grandstands, and on the field the anvils were hiding under plastic tarps.

A good many people would be staying away, and who could blame them? Tradition is a wonderful thing, but it is no fun to sit under an umbrella with the spray being blown back into your face just to watch something go bang.

And then, there they were, both wearing blue ponchos, both bent over ever so slightly. He had a walker. She had a white cane.

That is all you need hear to know that they were beautiful, they were dedicated and they *would be* on television later that night. I could have said they were worth talking to even if it wasn't my job to find someone beautiful and dedicated, and that would be true, but it would be less than honest.

So many of us would see the couple and think, "Gee, they look nice and, look, she is blind and he has trouble walking. I wonder how they got here and why she came to watch something that is known for a visual effect that she cannot see?" Most of us, including me, would think that, and then watch the show and forget about that achingly beautiful story off to the side.

I keep telling you that all you have to do to have a fantastic life is just talk to people, but there have been many times I have not done it. I have let the wonderful opportunity go by and sat in my seat and never said hello. When I do say hello my day is always better. When I don't, I later regret it. But still I frequently don't—a crazy human shortcoming.

But I was working on this day of the Anvil Battery salute, so I said hello. It was an opportunity.

"Hello, hate to bother you, but have you seen this before?"

Then I think, you idiot. She has a white cane.

"Also it's raining and I was wondering..." I said, trying to change the subject.

That is when kindness and understanding take over, not from me but from those I am speaking to. Have you noticed that when you are fumbling for something to say, or you say something stupid, someone will often help you get out of your jam by saying something that makes you feel less stupid? Don't ignore those people; they are the good teachers.

"We don't mind the rain, we never miss this," the woman said.

"Never?"

"Well almost never, not in more than sixty years," said the man.

"Actually, it's been more than that, sweetheart," said the woman. "Remember, I danced around the Maypole here when I was a girl."

You see? How could I have missed them? They have been here much more than me.

They settled onto the hard bench under the cover of the roof near home plate. When New West isn't firing off anvils here, they play baseball.

"Today is my birthday," said the woman.

Oh, super wonderful, I thought. A queen's birthday and the birthday of a blind woman both celebrated at the same time in the same place.

Her name is Helen and her husband is Alex. They have shared the same last name, Hughan, for sixty-five years.

"I tried to pick her up on a streetcar," said Alex. "My friend and I saw these two pretty girls and tried to talk to them, but they would have nothing to do with us."

Then fate and luck stepped in.

"We wound up at the same dance," he said.

"And it has been good since then," she added.

I asked why the rain did not keep them away. She said it was tradition, and I thought of the folks who started the tradition in spite of the downpour of official government rules against it. All strong people.

I asked, timidly, about her sight. She said she could not see me.

Then we stood for "O Canada."

The first bang went off a moment after that. The car alarms went off too. Some children cried. Helen laughed.

I asked if she enjoyed it as much with only hearing it.

"I saw it so many times I can still see it," she said.

Bang.

She laughed again.

Many seats were empty. Helen could not see that. She knew her seat and the one next to her were occupied. That is all that mattered.

Bang.

I asked if she knew when the explosions were coming. Everyone else could see and prepare themselves.

"I know," she said. "It's one minute between blasts. That's tradition."

Bang.

She and Alex jumped slightly out of their seats, as everyone did.

I asked Alex if he had wished her happy birthday yet. He looked at me as though there are strange questions in the world, but none as bad as that.

"Of course, first thing this morning."

But then he leaned over and said, "Happy birthday, sweetheart." And he kissed her.

Bang.

She smiled. He repeated the procedure, and then put his arm around her shoulder and held her tight while the man on the field with the long pole with the red-hot tip ran out to the pair of anvils. He squeezed her tighter. The man in the red jacket on the field with the long pole touched the spot with the gun powder.

Bang.

Helen and Alex jumped together, just slightly, really just moving their shoulders up, together.

I was standing far back now—this was their time, their tradition—but I could see him whisper something to her. Maybe happy birthday, maybe something else. She turned her face to him and smiled again, almost giggling like a young girl on a streetcar.

Bang. Jump. Smile.

There were twenty-one ear-hurting salutes. At the beginning the audience is warned to cover their ears and open their mouths. This is loud stuff.

Twenty-one cannon shots from a cannon that was not there honouring the birthday of a queen who was not there.

Bang.

And twenty-one explosions celebrating the birthday of a woman who was there, at least according to Alex, who still held her tightly.

Bang.

And for Helen, well, she saw the whole thing. She saw the proud New West folks loading the cannon with powder. She saw the defiant New West folks blowing apart the anvils. She saw the little girl in the white dress dancing around the Maypole.

Bang.

She saw her first year here with her new name, sitting next to the fellow who tried to pick her up on a streetcar.

Bang.

She saw her children and her grandchildren.

Bang.

And then they stood and sang "God Save the Queen."

We said goodbye. Then we watched the two of them, Alex with his walker and Helen with her cane, leave the stadium. They walked home. They told us where they were going, and I counted the streets. They walked home twenty-one blocks, in the rain.

Love Your News Deliverer

Love comes, love blooms, love goes. Read all about it. Love stories. Every newspaper will have one love story in every issue. It might be about a baseball player loving his glove, or it might be an anniversary that has a number larger than most people's age, but it will be there—if only you could find the paper. Where the heck did he leave it this morning?

That was Del Dimock's problem. She has the warm smile of friends of mine who are of East Indian descent and who came from the West Indies, except she is from Lynn Valley in North Vancouver. She has lived there most of her life, but she still had the same wonderful smile, except when she was hunting in the dark and the rain for her newspaper. She complained a few times, but nothing happened.

"Then suddenly it was all better," she said. "Look, the paper was propped up against my door jam every morning, just like this."

She showed us how it was leaning against the door frame, dry and waiting for her. She just had to reach out without stepping out.

Then Del did something kind. She called the newspaper and told them about the good service and also wrote a note thanking the delivery person.

"The next day I got back a note thanking me for my note."

That is how kindness grows and how it makes you feel good. Obviously the person who got the note was happy and the note in return made Del feel good. Not a bad return for investing a scrap of paper and a tiny bit of ink.

Time passed and Del left another note because her paper was always in the same spot. Consistency is a good thing.

A day later she got a note in return, again thanking her.

Del left another note talking about the weather and wishing her delivery person a good day off at the end of the week.

Over the next few months the notes went back and forth, two people becoming friends, with Del not knowing the other's name, or even gender. The return notes were signed, "Your delivery person."

"But I guessed she was a woman because the notes were tender and I could not see a fellow being so good with the paper."

I was hurt hearing that, but she was probably right.

Then the delivery person signed her name. Anna.

"I knew it, I knew it," she said.

She left some chocolates for Anna. She got a thank you.

And then one morning the paper was flat out, lying on the porch nowhere near the door.

Anna must be off today, Del thought. The next day the same thing. By the third day Del wrote a note asking about Anna and if anything had happened to her.

A note the next morning in rough handwriting said, "I am Gary. I am Anna's husband. Anna can't deliver the paper for a while. She's having a baby."

Oh joy, oh good feelings. Del was so excited. Her own very special newspaper delivery lady named Anna was having a baby. This is great. Except she had never seen Anna.

A few weeks later there was a knock on Del's door. She opened it. She knew, without asking, without talking. She knew instantly. There were just the two of them, with a proud smile on one of them and a cooing from the other. She knew.

"Oh, Anna, oh, so beautiful," she said.

Anna Cruz is from the Philippines. She and her husband are working hard to get somewhere in life, and in this new large country they now have one very close new friend. When I saw them, Del was standing in her doorway holding Anna's baby and Anna was standing by her side. The newspaper she had delivered was still leaning against the door frame. No love story in the paper would come close to that.

Horseshoe King

He did not have time to talk, not right now. He was taking aim.

"Just a minute," he said. His voice was sandy, sort of rough and gravely, but still smooth to the touch.

He dropped his right arm and with a swing forward he let go a large, steel horseshoe. It made one slow tumble in the air, and then clang, it hit the steel spike.

"Ha," he said.

"Now can we talk?"

"Just a minute," he said.

He had another horseshoe in his hand. Same thing. Same aim, same swing, same release, same tumble, same clang.

"Ha," he said.

"Now?"

"OK, now, but I have to walk to the other side."

"I'll follow," I said.

Conversation with John Jones was not fluid. His throws were, his aim in life was, but not conversation.

He reached down with a wooden pole with a hook at the end and picked up one horseshoe, then the other.

"How long have you been doing this?" I asked.

"Just a minute," he said.

Same thing. Aim, swing, and then … impossible! He missed!

"Ha," he said.

"Do you always laugh?" I asked.

"That was not a laugh. Do you think I would laugh about that?"

John did not laugh when he missed. And he took his misses seriously. Even when he was practising, like now. This was the first time I met him.

We were wandering through Central Park in Burnaby looking for anything that would turn into something when we heard the clang. And then another clang. And then a pause, a long pause, and then a clang.

I did not know there was a horseshoe pitch in the park. This was twenty years ago and there was still time to learn things. We followed the clangs and there, hidden almost in the centre of the park, were two long rows of horseshoe pitches. There were about fifteen in all, and just one man throwing the curved pieces of steel.

"Can I ask you something?"

"Not now."

He wore work gloves, but the thumb and first two fingers of the glove on the right hand were completely worn through. I watched for a minute and it appeared that his thumb and first two fingers were the only parts of his hand that touched the steel. The gloves must have been a habit, even when they were not working as gloves.

"Now," he said.

He had picked up his horseshoes, which were painted red, and was walking back to the little shack that is the headquarters of the BC Horseshoe Association. He did not wait for me, he just walked off.

"What do you want?" He turned his head back to say that.

"Do you play here often?"

Now I can imagine how that question must have sounded. Now I understand, but at the time it must have been like meeting an old prime minister or president of a country and asking naively, "How long have you been interested in politics?"

You don't answer that. You ask for a different reporter.

"Long time," he said.

"How long."

The voice very annoyed now, like how could I not know that he was the most famous horseshoe thrower in British Columbia?

"Very long."

Instead of going into the clubhouse he stopped at the last pitch and took aim at the spike across the pitch forty feet away. He dropped his hand and swung forward and clang.

"Very long."

This guy I have to talk with, but he does not want to talk.

Clang.

"I started when I was young," he said.

It took a while to find out, but I learned that he started in his twenties. He was talking now. If you have patience you often get what you are seeking.

He started in Stanley Park at their tiny horseshoe pitch with borrowed horseshoes, and, clang, followed by clang. He had found his place on earth.

There were so many clangs over the next few years that he was banned, or at least he said he was banned, from Stanley Park by the other horseshoe throwers. He made his way to Burnaby where he continued with clangs.

That is when he started painting his horseshoes red, so they would not get mixed up with the others. "I can't throw someone else's shoes," he said. "They don't feel right."

The horseshoe people in Burnaby were kinder and took him in. That was a long, long time ago. John got a night job in a sawmill just so he could spend his days throwing horseshoes.

"I never missed a day," he said. He said that many times over the years that I occasionally visited him, "Never a day except for one day."

He always said that, and said it with regret in his voice.

Cameraman John McCarron, with whom I worked a great deal, would say, "If we have nothing, let's go see the horseshoe man."

He was always there. He was there on Thanksgiving, all by himself. He was there on other holidays. He was there in the rain. He was there in the snow. But then he had to dig around the spike to find it before he would throw his shoes.

There are now small roofs over some of the sand boxes where the shoes land, but not in the early days, not when John was playing and was the only one playing.

He never married. "I didn't have time for that," he said. He played. He did not go visiting. "No time for that." He played. He owned nothing except his old car and his horseshoes.

You are thinking obsessive and compulsive. Yes, of course. And the answer to that is, "So?" John played horseshoes and John was good.

"He shot forty to fifty percent," said Ed Cirrani, whom I met at the pitch almost as many times as John. Except Ed has a family and another life and always has time to talk.

"John was the best man at this game I have ever seen," he said.

"Is forty to fifty percent good?" I asked.

Ed looked at me the same way as John had when I asked if he had been playing for long.

"It is impossible," he said.

And then John died. He was eighty-six. He had been moved into a care home for the very end of his life, the only time he could not get to the pitch and play. The only other time was that one day he missed.

Long before the end I asked him about that.

"I stopped to pick up some bottles for a few pennies, and I missed a day here," he said. He hung his head. He was still sad about that.

"It's a shame what happened," said Ed. "When he went into the home they took away his car and sold it at auction. They didn't even look inside. His horseshoes were in the trunk. They were always there."

In the clubhouse John's picture is on the wall under a sign that says: BC Horseshoe Hall of Fame.

When I was looking at it there was no noise coming from outside. There were no clangs. Then Ed left me alone to look at the wall.

Clang.

Central Park and Love

David Oppenheimer was sad. He was a widower with four kids, which is not an easy life. He had enough money to hire a nurse to take care of them, but that was not enough.

Earlier in life he had come from Germany with little money. He and three of his brothers had gone to New Orleans looking for wealth or at least a job. David found one in the equivalent of a corner store. It was not what he had come to America for.

Then he and his brothers heard about the gold rush in British Columbia. They moved here and opened a few stores in Victoria to supply the miners. Then a few more around New Westminster, and suddenly the money started flowing in.

The wealth of gold mining is not so much in gold as in selling boots and gold pans to those who want to get rich quickly. It is slow, but it works.

They made more and more, and suddenly, or it seemed suddenly, David Oppenheimer the poor boy was a rich man.

He moved back and forth between Victoria with its elegant living and Vancouver with its muddy streets, if you could call them streets. It was a strip of undefined land between the slash of the forest and the road with wagons.

But he was here and he met a woman and had four children and was happy. And then his wife died.

It happens.

Years went by. He was a widower and he hired a nurse to tell bedtime stories and get his children dressed but there was something missing.

He was popular and someone said he should run for mayor. Mayor? He was having enough trouble being a father and a shopkeeper, but they talked him into it and there was an election and David Oppenheimer was very well liked and he won, with no one running against him. He became Vancouver's second mayor.

He was a German immigrant. He was Jewish. He was a widower. He was a shopkeeper. Now he was mayor, and there was no scandal. See, it is possible.

As mayor he said we need parks. And we need transportation. So he used some of the money he had made selling boots to miners and bought land and gave it to the city to make parks. Nice guy. And he encouraged others to make a ferry line that would cross Burrard Inlet. And he got others to start working on a streetcar system.

He was a good guy and hard-working, and on a trip to San Francisco he met a woman. She was beautiful and it was, well, you know, it was love at first glance.

She was from New York. She missed New York. She wanted to go back to New York. But she felt the heart beating and the fingers wrapping around fingers and she said yes to David. Her name was Julia Walters. David talked her into joining him and his four children in Vancouver.

"Where is that?"

"North of San Francisco."

"Further from New York?"

"Just a bit."

She came, they married, she became an instant mother, and David asked what she missed most about New York.

"The parks," she said. "The beautiful parks, especially the one in the centre of the city called Central Park."

David was now into his second term as mayor. He knew the lay of the land. He knew that to the south and east of the city was a hunk of property that had been used by the British Navy to cut trees to use as masts and spars for their ships. He knew that piece of land, now that it had no trees on it and was useless for the military, was being returned to the people of British Columbia.

He knew it would be a good park, at least some day, when the trees grew back.

He signed what he had to sign and proclaimed what he had to proclaim and then asked his bride to climb onto a buggy and he drove her to the south and east of the fast-growing city of Vancouver.

On a dirt road he stopped and helped her get down. Then he walked with her to a small clump of trees and bushes that had a cloth over a sign.

"Ready?" he asked.

She nodded.

He pulled off the cloth and there were the words *Central Park*.

"This is for you," he said.

They lived very happily for many years. She had one child, a daughter. He went on to a total of four terms as mayor and did much good for the city. He built an orphanage and helped build a synagogue and Vancouver's first Young Men's Christian Association, the YMCA. Not a bad guy.

He died at the too-early age of sixty-four, which was after Julia had passed away. At his request he was buried next to her in a cemetery in

New York, actually in Brooklyn, because when you are from Brooklyn, which is just across the East River from the famous Manhattan, you never lose your love for it.

The two of them are still there now, and Central Park has grown into a place of towering trees and horseshoe pitches.

It is funny that Burnaby was created after Central Park was created and the park was absorbed into the new city. It turned out to be on the boundary line between the two cities. It is not in the centre at all. If it was being named today it would probably be called Boundary Park.

But if you walk around its paths, just imagine Julia and David on their first visit. Imagine Julia saying she was in Central Park and David holding her hand. You can hear the clanging of horseshoes. You can hear the kids playing. You are now in the middle of New York, or anywhere you want to be, just like them.

Marathon Walkers

They were walking on the beach. Many people walk on the beach, but he had two canes. They were not the trendy ski poles that some people use for walking; they were canes, and they were sinking in the sand.

"Keep going, please," I thought. "Don't just walk out there for a few steps and then come back to the paved walkway. Stay out there, please."

I think many things when I see something I think is beautiful. I want it to go on. I want it to be an inspiration. I want it to be a work of art.

If he stayed on the sand he would be doing something courageous, something different. If he just went out there for a few steps and found it was too difficult I would understand, but he would be doing what most of us do, trying something hard and then retreating to something easy.

He stayed. He and his wife were walking on the sand. She was short and every strand of her hair blowing in the wind was white. He was tall and his hair was the same.

"Excuse me, it's none of my business," etc. You know my approach. "Why are you here?"

"We used to run here," he said.

And just at that moment a lunchtime running group passed by on the paved walkway.

"That was a long time ago," said his wife.

He said she was a marathoner. She had done many of those runs that make you curse them when you are still far from the end and make you swear you will never do it again. And then when you get very close to the end you hit what they say is the wall, the moment when you can't run any further. It happens in race after race, and again you swear you will never do this again.

And then you get excited when you start training for the next race, and you do it again, and again.

You do it until you get to a point when you cannot do it anymore.

"I've had two knee replacements," she said. "So I walk."

He has had one new knee, but he was ten years older than her and one knee plus a decade can slow you down.

They lived in Vancouver in the 1980s and '90s, and then moved to Cranbrook. They were just back for a visit and could not believe how things had changed. There were forests of condos where small apartment houses had been.

And there was public art where none had been.

"What are those things? The rings?" she asked.

"Engagement rings," I said. I am happy when I can tell someone something they don't know. "But when they put them up they had lights in the diamonds and the lights annoyed the people in the condos so they had to take the sparkle out of the rings."

They laughed, and the only sparkle I could see now was in their eyes.

"We did the New Year's Midnight Run on this beach," he said.

"We lived in Burnaby and my wife would run from home to Stanley Park, then around the park, then home." Alan was bragging about the woman with the white hair who was now his walking partner.

"We still go for walks," she said.

Four miles a day is their base stroll. "Sometimes a hike in the mountains," she added. "Sometimes six or eight miles. It feels good."

Another group of runners in shorts and baseball caps jogged by. It is good they run. It is good they have friends and do it together. There is everything right with them.

But it was better to be talking to a couple who were walking. The marathon is not twenty-six miles. It is twenty-six years, or longer. In truth, there is no finish line. The canes, the sand, are just part of the route. This couple were beautiful to watch. They were an inspiration.

And when we left them, they were back on the sand, walking.

Orphans' Fund Playland Picnic

The day was over, and we were just starting. That occasionally happens with me, with you, with life, but it doesn't mean it is over.

I do not mean to make light of being late. When you don't show up and other folks are waiting you become a pain. It is not fair to them and, when you get right down to it, you should always be fair.

But showing up late for something for yourself just means you are starting on a different schedule.

That is an involved way of saying the cameraman and I met very late in the day. It would not be easy to find something, get it inside the camera, then get it out and put the pieces together and then broadcast it into the firmament.

We were in the middle parking lot of the PNE, a nice place to meet because usually there is nothing going on and it is easy to park.

"Go."

"Which way?"

"Does it matter?"

It does not matter who said what. When you are late and directionless it does not matter which direction you take, so long as you go. He turned right.

Half a minute away, unknown to me or him, was the CKNW Orphans' Fund Annual Picnic at Playland. We could not hear or see it from where we met. There was only one problem: it was over.

Thousands of kids were pouring out of the gates and heading back to their buses.

Darn.

But no. Look at what they are carrying. Almost every one of them had a balloon, and most of the balloons were green, and if you stood back, as we were, it looked like a forest of floating latex bouncing above the heads of an army of laughing and giggling kids.

Beautiful.

"Let us stand back and take pictures." One of us said that, the brighter one, the one with the camera.

His name is Tony Clark and he is the cameraman who was in the book *Getting to the Bubble*. He knows how one thing will lead to another and then another and you never know where you are going to end up when you start out for anything. That makes life, and the day, interesting.

The last time we met he told me about a lacrosse game his sons had played and the other team had been very rough and one of the kids on his team had been taken to a hospital and others were badly hurt. The other team was encouraged to be rough by their coach, and out of this had come official complaints and suspensions. This is a league of ten- and eleven-year-olds.

Stories like that hurt.

But now we were looking at balloons, which have a magical way of removing bad thoughts from your mind.

We got closer and I tried to talk to a large boy, maybe the same age as Tony's sons, about his balloon.

"Is that fun, that balloon?" I asked.

But there was no answer. Just eyes staring at me. Then he jerked his balloon down and watched it go up again to the end of the string and he laughed.

Of course. The Orphans' Fund Picnic is not about orphans any longer. There are no more orphanages as there were when the Fund was started fifty years ago. At that time the poor kids always came from the orphan homes and would not get a chance to ride on the roller coaster or have hot dogs if it was not for the radio station's kindness.

And at that time we did not know much about these other kids, the ones in wheelchairs and those who could not speak or clap their hands together. You did not know about them unless there was one in your family, and then you either kept him or her inside or sent him or her to an institution where he or she was kept inside.

Unless you carried the ache of one in your heart, they did not exist. They were not in schools, they were not on public transportation, they were not in churches or synagogues or mosques. They were not in Playland.

Times change. We grow up, thankfully. The way we deal with life changes, thankfully. Now orphans are usually adopted or live in small government homes until they are adopted. There are no more orphanages. And the orphans that we knew as a "special" group of kids have been replaced by the special children, with needs, with wheelchairs, with white canes and with ramps to get them into the family van.

And now *they* get into the vans and buses to go to Playland, at least once a year.

There were lots of pictures of balloons and kids playing with them, along with some blue ices on a stick that made the kids' teeth blue.

"Why are your teeth blue?" I asked one girl who did not seem to have special needs.

I know what she was thinking: why is an adult who is supposedly smart, because all adults are supposedly smart, asking such a dumb question?

"It is because I am eating blue ice," she said. But it was the look on her face that said, "I hope I don't grow up to be as dumb as this man" that was a highlight of the story.

However, the true high point was a combination of two things that came together. One was that I believe balloons should be set free. After they have brought laughter and bounces on the head that do not hurt, the little fingers should loosen around the string and everyone will watch.

The balloon will do what we all want to do. It will fly, and it will be free. I don't know if a five-year-old has that concept, but I have never seen a five-year-old or a sixty-five-year-old who will take their eyes off a balloon that is going up and up into whatever is up there.

But these kids were holding on tightly. I looked up, and saw nothing. Then I looked down and saw a girl in a wheelchair leaving. She was holding a balloon and being pushed by her mother.

"Hello," etc.

"Her name is Emma and she had a wonderful day," said her mother.

Emma sort of smiled. Emma squirmed in her chair that was more than a chair. It was her world.

"We went on the roller coaster."

"You *did*?"

Okay, I am a person of few experiences. I could not believe that a girl who could not walk or even sit up could go on one of the world's scariest rides. I was thinking how? How could you hold on, how could she hold on, how could you both survive? Do kids like this really go on rides like that? Do they really have fun? But those are the thoughts of someone prejudging, and in every case they hurt.

"Of course."

That was all she had to say and she helped me grow up, just a bit.

"And she loves her balloon," said her mother, who tapped it on Emma's face very gently.

Emma was fourteen. She has a rare disease that has too many letters to try to write. The name of the disease doesn't matter. It is bad. I thought she was nine or ten years old.

Her mother started to push Emma and her wheelchair up a ramp into the back of her van. The licence plate said: EMMA.

Tony was taking a picture of the struggle to get her into the vehicle. And then I looked up. A green balloon was floating up, overhead. I do not know where it came from or which kid let it go. I don't know if it was let go on purpose or some kid had said, darn, there goes my balloon. I only know that as Emma was being pushed up the ramp, a green balloon was flying free over her.

Tony got a picture of it. The van, the ramp, the wheelchair, the little girl and the balloon. If you had been standing there you might have seen something else, something seen on television later that night. Just before Emma was slid into the steel box, she looked up at the balloon. Near the bottom of one picture was the face of the little girl. Near the top was the balloon flying overhead. Over the picture I said, "The balloon and Emma looked at each other. They'd both had a good day."

It didn't matter that we had missed all the fun and pictures of the rides. It didn't matter that we were late. We saw the beginning of a beautiful memory.

Orphans' Fund Picnic Number Two
(which was actually Number One)

A long time ago, before any of the children who were at Playland in the previous story, in fact before some of their parents, were born, I was at the same place for the same reason and something similar happened, something amazing.

Orphans' Fund Picnic, 1977. The most significant thing about that date for me was that television news was done on 16-millimetre film. It travelled from a reel at one end of the camera to a reel at the other end, and it was expensive. Everyone was urged to use as little as possible to save money. It could easily break. It had to be taken out of the camera in a black bag so that light would not touch it. It had to be processed—developed, then passed through a fixing bath and dried—before it could be used. It was a pain.

I had done a story much like the one you've just read, except it was entirely different. We showed some rides and some cotton candy and some clouds and some very happy kids, including some with Down's syndrome who were mixed in with the orphans.

Later in the edit room we were running behind schedule. We were late, just like in the previous story. The editor, a tall woman from Austria, and I were working as fast as we could but the minutes were passing.

She had cut, physically, literally cut the film in strips and was taping them together. That is why we still call editing cutting. "Did you cut your story yet?" There is no cutting now, there are no moving parts now, but we still say we are cutting a story and, of course, we are still late.

This was an age before most special effects. There was no practical way to have slow motion. The film ran through the camera and the projector at one speed.

Once I worked with a cameraman who tried to show an older woman running around a track in slow motion. He opened the back of his camera and where it had a setting for film speed he slowed down the dial. Logically that would have worked, except in reality when he slowed down the film in the camera it ran through the projector at normal speed.

Think about that for a second. If it was recorded slow and run back normally, that means it was projected as going faster, so the grey-haired woman, who was also blind, was shown on television as almost flying around the track.

"Is she really going that fast?" I was asked. "That looks like an Olympic runner, not a seventy-year-old woman."

I answered with one of those stupid looks that means please do not ask me.

So slow motion was not big in the days of film. But at that moment, in an edit room with a razor blade attached to a small device for cutting the film, we were in high-speed worry. The first two minutes of the story had already been put on a large reel that was in the projection room. We were assembling the last twenty or thirty seconds of the story that would go on what was called a Special Reel.

That would be one that was put on a second projector and started up just at the time that the first reel of film was coming to an end.

I had already recorded the closing comments on an audio cassette that would be played simultaneously with the film.

"How long was that segment?" I was thinking when I was in the audio booth. "It's thirty seconds, right, yes, thirty seconds. I'm sure of that."

So I recorded comments that went on for half a minute.

Back in the edit room the lovely tall editor had finished the final bit of film and had it on the Special Reel. I grabbed it and ran upstairs to the projection room. The first two minutes of the story were already on the air.

A fellow in the room grabbed the reel from me and slid it onto a second projector. We were down to fifteen seconds before the second projector would have to be turned on. There was no time to thread the end of the film onto a take-up reel.

There was a quick, synchronized countdown as the first projector ran out of film and the second was started. "Three, two, one, go."

And it was perfect. The second reel of film with a picture of a girl with Down's syndrome playing with a balloon came up at just the exact right second.

Sigh.

"Twenty seconds to go," said the projectionist.

"Twenty seconds? But I have thirty seconds of words," I said.

Without hesitation, without a script or direction from a director, without deliberation, the projectionist grabbed the dial on the projector that controlled the speed and started slowing down the picture. He could only do it a slight bit or you would start seeing the lines between the frames of the pictures and, worse, the oncoming film would jumble up, like the back of a line suddenly bunching up if the head of the line slowed down. The film would jam. That would be television disaster.

And then, with less than five seconds of film left and almost seven or eight seconds of words still to come, he hit the stop button but left the bulb burning. The picture froze on the screen. It would last only a few seconds before the heat from the bulb would set it on fire.

The words that I said are forgotten. They had something to do with the power or beauty of life or kids. I have no idea what I said, but the image was a close-up of the little kid who had the face of an angel and the unfairness of bad genes. It lasted long enough for the words to finish, and then it was over. The projectionist hit the start button and the end of the film ran out on the floor. One or two more seconds and the film would have been burning and a fire extinguisher would have cancelled the rest of the show.

In the studio, the fellows who manually operated the big cameras were hiding their eyes. One, and then the other two, started to applaud. I was told that had never happened. The anchors were holding back tears and were thankful a commercial had come on.

CKNW used that closing picture for their advertising and promotion for the Orphans' Fund for the following year.

None of it was planned.

No Christmas Without It

"We've got to sing the Twelve Days of Christmas. The time is *now*."

Rosie was shouting *now*, but few could hear her. The noise in the party was so loud you could only hear the person next to you.

"What? I can't hear you." I said.

"I *said*," said Rosie, shouting the word *said*, "It's time to sing."

"No, I still can't hear you," I said.

It was so noisy you couldn't even hear the fire trucks passing by.

Wait, the trucks are turning at the corner outside the house. Two, three. You can only see their flashing lights on the ceiling because it is too crowded to see through the windows.

"Is this house on fire?" someone shouted, but you couldn't hear her either unless you were right next to her.

I *was* standing next to her, but Rosie was on the other side of me shouting, "*Now!* The Twelve Days of Christmas."

But before the singing: "Something's burning down the street."

I could hear that because someone had opened the door and let out some of the noise. The door was right next to the band, which had a singer, a great many instruments, a microphone and a speaker, but that was still the quieter part of the home.

Now the door was open and someone with a saxophone had joined the jam session. That made three guitars (one of them electric), an electric keyboard, drums, two rattles filled with beans, a tambourine and a sax. Most of these musicians have made an income from playing, so they actually do make music—very good music.

It is the music of the first Saturday in December, the Bread Party. Ingrid Rice, who draws editorial cartoons for scores of community newspapers across the country, likes bread, and starting in the summer she bakes twenty to thirty different kinds. Some are sweet, some are savoury, some have seeds, some coconut, some have herbs, some spices, some are from recipes, some from her imagination. It is like the music.

She freezes the loaves, and early on the first Saturday in December she takes them out of the cold and spreads them around a large table. Her guests are asked to bring some spread for the bread.

Ingrid and Bob York also have guinea pigs—many guinea pigs. They are not normal people, if normal people are people who have one guinea pig for their child's pet. Ingrid and Bob have a dozen guinea pigs, sometimes more, all for themselves.

The guinea pigs run free in their living room. Yes, I know what you're thinking, and you are right. There is a large sheet of plastic covering the floor. If you are visiting and sit on the couch, there is a good chance a guinea pig will crawl out between your feet. Yes, again I know what you are thinking, and again you are right. You will make immediate mention of the animal between your shoes and you'll raise your feet off the floor and spill the wine that's in a glass in your hand

and your pants will be wet, on which you will also comment, loudly and profanely.

But there will be more wine and more guinea pigs and you will laugh and have a good time and get used to little furry animals that look like loveable rats with no tails scurrying around the floor while you try to speak of politics or social affairs.

Of course, it is impossible to talk of anything other than guinea pigs while they climb over your shoes, but it is nice to think that a normal conversation could go on if not for the guinea pigs.

I have written about them before, six books ago, and they have been on television. One of the stories was when Ingrid invented a wheelchair for guinea pigs. The creatures sometimes develop an ailment that results in degenerative hips, which makes walking difficult. She strapped little chariots with wheels under their little bottoms and then the guinea pigs could run and keep up with each other, making them happy little guinea pigs as they slipped out between feet in front of the couch.

Another time I did a television story about Ingrid and Bob's grass-cutting friends. You mow your lawn. Ingrid and Bob feed their lawn to their "pigs." They have built a large square cage with no bottom. The guinea pigs go into the cage and can't believe their luck. They are in guinea pig heaven. They have grass. Sex would be the ultimate heaven, but even Ingrid and Bob have sense. They have only female pigs, so grass becomes the heaven.

The pet pigs that are not really pigs feast on the soft, usually moist, green slivers of lunch and dinner until they have chewed up every last strand. Then their loving keepers move the cage. Oh, my heavens. Paradise has been born again. More grass.

The pigs eat and the grass is cut and Ingrid and Bob watch from chairs in the garden on which they sip lemonade and read newspapers. Occasionally one of them rises to move the cage and more grass is cut and it is replaced by fertilizer. What more could anyone ask?

But I have not told you about the first Saturday of December when the bread comes out of the freezer and is placed on a table and people come to hear the music and shout to each other. The one mandatory part of the night (besides eating bread and marvelling at all the guinea pigs, which are not wandering the floor tonight) is singing the Twelve Days of Christmas. Every year an old cardboard box comes out of hiding and out of it come twelve signs with handles. The first sign says "A Partridge In A Pear Tree." The second sign: "Two Turtle Doves." You know the rest. It is cheerful, it is fun, and it is one of the best songs of Christmas because twelve people get leading roles.

But first we have to check the fire down the street. Most people at the party are the type who don't want to be accused of chasing fire engines. Too grown up, too intellectual for that kind of fun. Either that or it is because they are in the kitchen with the guinea pigs who are in their three-story condo cage to keep them safe. The cage has a sheet over it and plates of smoked salmon and bread on top.

"Do you know what's under that sheet?" someone who has been here before always shouts to someone who has never been to the party before.

"No," the newcomer shouts back.

The veteran whispers inaudibly into her ear, "Guinea pigs," and then lifts a corner. The young innocent newbie's eyes open wider, then wider. She is now a veteran, and she removes her plate from the top of the cloth-covered condo and tries to slip into the crowd with the news that they are not alone.

The kitchen is like a subway car at rush hour but with wine and bread and guinea pigs and so many people shouting "What did you say" that you cannot hear the music that is ten steps away. And you cannot hear the sirens that are outside, so it is probably not fair to label the guests as intellectuals who do not wish to be seen watching firemen at work. They are ordinary, good, curious people like everyone here, except they are caught in a separate universe or possibly a fourth dimension, and so they don't know the outside offers the peace of a burning house.

There is always a simple answer to be found if you believe you will find it. The fire is in the chimney of a house down the street and is out before we (even me, who makes a living off watching firemen and fires) get outside. Despite the fire truck engines and the shouts of the firemen and the radios in the trucks, it is so quiet outside, except for the noise coming from that house on the corner.

We go back inside. Rosie has given out the signs that have pictures drawn on them of a Turtle Dove, Five Gold Rings, etc., etc.

We begin singing.

First day, Partridge.

Second day, Doves.

Third day, silence.

Repeat:

"On the third day of Christmas my true love sent to me ..."

Silence.

The din of the entire room has stopped, except for the dozen or so people who can now *finally* get to talk to whomever they are talking to. Actually, the dozen or so talkers are quite loud, now that almost everyone else isn't. Except for them, there is silence.

"Where is the Third Day?"

"She's out having a smoke."

"She can't be smoking during the third day," Ingrid said emphatically. "We need a fill-in Third Day."

Someone raises a hand.

We sing again.

"On the third day of Christmas my true love sent to me ..."

A newcomer holds up three fingers.

"Three French Hens."

It is working even without the smoker.

On the fourth day:

"Four Calling Birds."

Totally no one knows what a Calling Bird is, but we sing it and the fellow holding the sign is doing his part holding the sign up high. He is very good looking and very tall. We like seeing the sign.

On the fifth day:

Now this is the big one. This is the prize. The person who gets the Fifth Day is the chosen one because they have Five Gold Rings, which takes longer to sing than Three French Hens and Four Calling Birds lumped together.

A beautiful, tall woman holds up Five Gold Rings and sings.

But at the same time the very good-looking and very tall fellow with the Four Calling Birds holds up his sign cheering on Five Gold Rings. He is so happy seeing her on centre stage that he wants to applaud, but he has his sign in one hand so he holds it up for her like a bouquet of roses.

He is in love with Five Gold Rings. She is in love with him.

She is wearing a gold ring with a sparkling diamond on the third finger of her left hand, which means they are totally in love but are not yet married (which in a few years can sometimes put a strain on love).

But you cannot see her Five Gold Rings sign because his Four Calling Birds is in front of it, waving with joy and admiration, which are good things to have when you are in love.

"I can't see the Five Gold Rings sign," someone shouts, but it is not heard.

The song continues with Partridges and Leaping Lords and Maids A-Milking, but every time Gold Rings comes up, Calling Birds hides them. Calling Birds is beaming. Gold Rings is looking longingly at Calling Birds. Calling Birds can see only Gold Rings.

In some choruses the only one singing Five Gold Rings is the tall beauty with the diamond ring because no one else can see her sign.

She does not notice this. She only has eyes for Calling Birds while she is singing about Gold Rings.

But the ultimate moment, more important than Gold Rings, more important than Swans Swimming, is the Twelve Drummers Drumming.

Everyone waits for this because by the time you get to the twelfth day you are tired of singing about birds and maids and dancers, and here at last come Twelve Drummers Drumming.

But again, as with French Hens, the drums are silent.

"Oh, come on," said Ingrid. "There's got to be a drummer here. We can't have another smoker."

The drummer in the actual band over in the next room looks up, and then down, as if to say, "Don't pick me, please, don't pick me. I'm just the drummer, who is not the flashiest one in the band but I always get the girls and I don't know why but I am not going to question it."

In relative terms, the room is again silent. Ingrid is ticked off—and a ticked-off Ingrid is not something to trifle with.

"Who is the Twelfth Day of Christmas?"

I had pity for the person. They would not enjoy a thirteenth day.

"Whoops," said Rosie whose head was inside a large, long cardboard box. "I forgot to give out the Twelve Drummers Drumming sign."

"Here," she said, handing it to a newcomer.

"Sing," said Rosie.

"Sing now," said Ingrid.

"I can't sing," said the Twelve Drummers Drumming sign holder.

"Sing, sing," said a few people next to the drummer who was not drumming.

"On the twelfth day of Christmas my true love gave to me, Twelve Drummers Drumming."

It was true. He could not sing.

"Eleven Pipers Piping,"

And on to

"Nine Lords A-Leaping,"

"Eight Maids A-Milking."

And "Five Gold Rings," whose face was still being hidden behind the love of Four Calling Birds.

It was the way it was meant to be.

Merry Christmas.

The Left–Behind Angel

S he was about ten, her older sister maybe three years more advanced. She was being admonished in Russian, or maybe it was Albanian, by her father who was large and unbending.

Inside Canadian Tire, two weeks before Christmas, she was holding tightly onto a plastic container in which there was an angel. Its wings were folded, there was a glow on its face and I think there was a halo resting on the doll's head, but I could not be sure because the arms of the little girl were wrapped around the container.

I moved on, looking for some plastic sheets to cover my windows. They don't look so good, but they work as well as double-paned glass and instead of paying $400 a window I pay only $4. I know I can't open the windows once they are taped and sealed into place, but breathing isn't everything.

When I was going to the cash register to pay, I saw the little girl by herself in the middle of an aisle. It being absolutely none of my business, I walked into it. Or at least I walked halfway into it. I stood pretending to look at some decorations on a shelf about ten steps away and without turning my head I moved my eyes and watched.

She hugged the plastic container and she spoke to the angel. She was whispering, I don't know in what language. Then she cried and kissed the top of the plastic and put it back on the shelf and walked away. She did not turn back.

I saw the price was $24.95 and knew what the father had been saying. Price tags have no language barriers.

The angel looked out through the plastic. The little girl was gone.

Later that night she would have cried again when she went to bed. I don't have to guess at that. You know it is true.

And in her mind she had the angel. She could see it. She could feel it. And she could talk to it.

Sometime soon one of her friends will be talking about Guardian Angels and the little girl will say she believes in them and that she has one and she will describe what her special angel looks like. She will say her angel's wings are folded and her face has a glow. And she will know whether her angel has a halo. She will know because she has seen her angel and she will say her angel is always with her.

In twenty or thirty years' time, another little girl will talk to her mother about angels and her mother will tell her a story about an angel in a plastic container that turned into a real angel. The little girl will grow up believing that she, too, has a special angel, because her mother told her so.

There is no right or wrong in saying no to spending $24.95. If you can't afford it, if you don't think it is a wise way to spend what you don't have then there is no question. The angel goes back to the shelf. But if you are ten and you believe in angels, there is no way it is going to stay there.

The Christmas Market

H e was weaving and bobbing his head.

"Please, Georgie, stand still for just a second."

His mother was trying to get his picture. She raised the camera but he moved. He turned around again. She lowered the camera.

"Please, just for a second, please help Mommy."

She raised the camera, but he turned around yet again. He had a silly grin, almost like he was playing a game, but I didn't think he was. He held a white cane but he was not using it. His feet were not moving, but his head and shoulders were not stopping.

Behind him was the carousel. It was a turning mass of horses rising and falling, and his mother wanted to get a picture of him standing in front of it.

You could see, anyone could see, that he was the word we do not use any more—retarded. But he was not that. He was mentally challenged. And he was blind. And I could also tell, because I had seen him earlier with his mother while she tried to get him to eat a German sausage on a bun, that he was mute.

The challenge was for his mother, and she had obviously spent a long time trying to deal with it. He was about eighteen and was taller and much heavier than her.

To help him eat, she tore off a piece of sausage and put it in his fingers. He took a bite and she used that moment to take a bite of her own sausage. Then she tore off a piece of the bun and gave it to him. He put it to his lips but then, in some kind of annoyance, dropped it. It fell on the ground.

He did not shake his head to say no—he did not have that much communication—but it was clear he wanted more of the greasy, tasty sausage. She gave him another piece of that and grabbed a quick bite of her own. Not once did she look annoyed or angry or frustrated. She looked at him with love and sadness.

But that was earlier. Now back at the carousel she raised her camera again, but he turned his head. Of course he turned around. He could hear what was behind him, could hear the carousel that was playing a sweet bit of something that was probably Mozart condensed and interpreted through some electronic recordings to make it suitable for a three-minute ride on plastic horses.

She wanted his picture with the carousel behind him, something he would never in his entire hard and isolated life understand. She had so much warmth and kindness in her face and her words. You could tell in once glance that her patience was long and that the anger and frustration threshold were way in the distance.

I knew she wanted the picture to show to someone so they could see that Georgie had not only been to the market but he had enjoyed it. He just wanted to listen.

I walked on with my wife, looking at the Christmas decorations for sale and trying to figure out which of the sausages and schnitzels

I wanted to eat. I finally chose one that looked good and asked for it with sauerkraut.

"It does not come with sauerkraut. The pork chop comes with sauerkraut."

"You're kidding," I said.

"No," was the emphatic answer from the man selling the sausages and the pork chops with sauerkraut.

"That's crazy," I said.

"We only have enough sauerkraut for the pork chops," he said.

"Never mind, skip it," I said and went off hungry and annoyed, because how can you sell sausages and not have enough sauerkraut to put on them? This is no way to run a hot dog stand, even if you are not selling hot dogs.

But most of all, I did not get what I wanted, and for at least four minutes my night was crushed. "All I wanted was sauerkraut and they wouldn't give it to me," I told my wife.

"Well, eat something else," she said.

I thought, she doesn't understand. But how could she not understand that all I wanted was some simple sauerkraut and I could not get it. Was that such a big deal? It's a German market, right? They should have sauerkraut for the sausages.

I got a pretzel and mustard. They had that. Actually, I grew up eating pretzels and mustard in New York. It's kind of soul food of the street and I was much happier with the taste than if I had had a sausage and sauerkraut. And it was cheaper. So I came out ahead.

Going to a German Christmas market is not as simple as it might sound. There are so many cross-references going on in the heads of basically everyone there. There were the people lining up for the apple cider mixed with wine. They were saying how good that tasted and they were getting back in line for a second cup even though one cup was way more expensive than apple cider and wine should cost.

We were told that rum was added to the wine that was added to the cider, which made the customers come back even more quickly. And then we watched the customers buying more food, which is what you do when you drink apple cider with wine and rum. Germans are very smart.

And inside the large tent that held hundreds of various German Christmas tree decorations with large prices there were very nice-looking German young people who spoke impeccable English helping the customers who were carrying cups of apple cider with wine and rum. "Can I help you?" Of course, in this condition everyone needs help. Germans are very, very smart.

This is not meant as any kind of criticism. That was marketing and customer relations and low pressure salesmanship, and it was working brilliantly. And everyone was having an experience while they were taking out their credit cards.

And over there, on the other side of the tent, was Georgie's mother trying to look at some of the decorations. She was also trying to keep Georgie from banging into things, grabbing things and getting in the way of other shoppers who were carrying straw baskets with decorations in one hand and cups of apple cider in the other.

It was crowded. They could not look where they were going. They were looking at the decorations and sipping and looking at the prices and listening to the young Germans and talking to their friends and talking on their cell phones.

Georgie's mother tried to pick up one fragile-looking angel made of wood but Georgie lurched away and she grabbed him and put the decoration down. She tried again, but he turned the other way. I watched her lead him out of the tent. She should not have brought him in there, she was probably thinking.

We stayed in the tent and bought some things that looked very nice but would maybe disappear on a tree in the living room, and some things that were given to people after Christmas because we did not see them before Christmas and they would say they are very nice and would put them away to bring out next year, if they remembered.

We left the tent and got a couple of cups of the apple cider with wine and rum. We fooled them. We shopped first. Then we listened to a choral group singing German Christmas carols. It was really very lovely. We told each other what a good night it was and then we left.

We passed the carousel. Georgie was sitting on one of the horses that was going up and down. He looked terrified when it went up and giggled when it came down. His mother was standing next to him holding on to one of his arms.

With her other hand she held the camera and each time the horse went down she took a picture. Angels go to markets. And carry cameras. And have patience.

Olympic Yoga vs.
Olympic Hockey Watching

"You had a stray thought," said the judge.

"I humbly protest that accusation. I had an *expanded* thought," said the athlete, quietly.

The athlete was on the mat with her right leg pointed out, her head pointed up, her left arm pointed down and her right arm tied in a knot behind her back.

The Five Rings were hanging from the ceiling. The judges were considering.

"Stray thought. I could see it in the flicker of her eyelid."

"She said 'expanded' thought," said another judge.

"Is 'expanded thought' an evolution of 'stray thought' or is it an aberration?" asked the third judge, who was from India and was sitting in lotus on the table.

Yoga, as you may know, may become an Olympic sport. True. Honest. We do not kid about things that mean so much to so many.

Of all the thousands, tens of thousands, of mostly women who go to the gym with their yoga mats rolled up behind them in their shoulder bags, one or two may achieve the gold medal for doing... nothing. But doing nothing with great elegance, grace and poise.

The athletes will be judged on their meditation—competitive meditation—and expanded consciousness. No kidding. This is right from the *New York Times*. Meditation will be judged along with patience and, of course, the ultimate S-T-R-E-T-C-H, which will precede the post-competitive stretch.

The athlete being questioned on her stray thought was now into her stretch.

"She could be in expanded thought right now," said a judge, "And in that case her 'expanded thought' could get extra points."

"But is 'Thought' the same as 'Consciousness'?" said the judge from India, who then went on to speak of the consciousness of thought, as described in the original Sanskrit.

Meanwhile, the athlete being questioned waited patiently, because patience is one of the criteria.

I have no argument with yoga as part of the Olympics. I have trouble tying my shoelaces. I don't care if the Games include golf or bowling—we are an evolving society—but I have a friend, Karl, who says that if Yoga can be a sport, then so can Beer and Hockey.

"I can sit in a perfect trance for half a period, not moving anything, not a finger, not a toe, and definitely not an eyelid."

That is at least twenty minutes of total, absolute, expanded consciousness. That would be awesome for a yogi to accomplish while in a stance that was designed to promote healthy blood flow. Imagine the TV-Hockey-Fan-Athlete doing the same while slouched on a couch in a position that would inhibit not only his circulation but his breathing as well. There is a true competitor.

And when the beer is finished and the goal is scored against his team, look at how that empty can is crushed. We have added an aggression clause to the sport. Unbeatable, unbelievable: the gold medal for watching an entire game with hardly taking a breath and crushing five cans.

Karl has spent his life training for this. Age and weight and team affiliation offer no restrictions. Bring on the competition, whomever they cheer for, he says.

And here is where it gets interesting. If there are tens of thousands of potential yoga athletes, there are millions of hockey watchers. And Canada would knock the socks off every other country on the planet. The gold medal for the slouch on the couch. There is not a stray thought in his head.

Whatever Happened to Spitballs?

I was talking about the old days with my ninety-four-year-old friend Harold Wolverton. He has *really* old days, but we settled for something we both had in school that doesn't exist any longer. Spitballs.

That is a problem. Where did they go? There are no more spitballs. You can go through an entire life now and never shoot a spitball at anyone or even see one flying across a classroom.

I know they are disgusting and slimy and germ covered, but that's what is good about them. The perfect unseen stealth weapon. But they have slipped out of life like the Twinkie.

Now mothers are trying to get their kids to eat better, but when I was young we lived on Twinkies. And Coke. And bubble gum. Sure, our teeth were bad. Sure, we were hyper. But it was our tradition. Like spitballs.

Before the knowledge disappears forever, here is the formula. You may be the only person left knowing it.

Rip a small piece of paper off the end of a newspaper.

What's a newspaper?

It is, or was, a large piece of cheap paper covered with words that told you about what was going on in the world. You got a new one every day.

Do you mean you had to wait a full day to find out what was happening?

No, you could turn on your television and find out what was up every couple of hours, but you could not make a spitball out of a TV.

Let me get this straight. You had to wait more than an hour to learn what's up?

Well, an hour was pretty fast, but I know your tiny computer tells you everything every minute.

No, not every minute. Every second. Even faster. I could not live if I didn't know what was happening now. Not five minutes from now, but *now!*

Stop, my turn again. Very simply, you cannot make a spitball from a hand-held computer. You need paper.

But this is a paperless world. We do not kill trees just to have something on which to record words that we won't read and to then throw away.

Well, just for the sake of education, historical information, about your ancestors such as your parents, please get me a piece of paper.

From where?

I don't care where you find it. Look through your mother's drawers. Maybe she has some old love letters.

Why would anyone write their love on a piece of paper? What would you do with it after you were no longer in love?

Burn them, for god's sake.

You don't have to get mad. I was just wondering what you did with love letters after you stopped being in love.

Well, maybe you never stopped.

I don't stop. I am on e-love and have a new love every week.

Lucky you. Do you have a bus pass? That's made of paper.

I have one, but it is in my cell phone. I just wave that at the scanner on the bus.

Grocery list?

Cell phone.

Birthday card?

Cell phone.

Writing paper?

Don't write.

Homework?

On my tablet.

Label off a CD?

Download tunes.

Alright, do you have any paper in your life?

Toilet paper.

No. Won't do. Okay, here is a page from my notebook.

What's a notebook?

It is a small pad of paper with a spiral binding and you keep it in your pocket to make notes on.

I do that on my iPad.

Suppose the batteries die and you have to make a note. Here's a pen. Let's see you write "How To Make A Spitball."

My batteries are extremely long lasting, and there is a solar power adaptor.

Please write.

I didn't learn how. I can print, but I haven't done that since grade two.

Tear a strip off the paper.

Can it be recycled?

It's only a tiny piece of paper.

But if everyone did this it could become an ecological disaster.

Just tear off a strip.

Then what?

Put it in your mouth.

What? How did your generation survive?

Just do it.

Yuck.

Now roll it into a ball.

But it's covered with spit.

Perfect.

Now you can either put it into a plastic straw and shoot it or, in an emergency, just throw it.

Why?

So you can hit someone.

Why?

Because that's what spitballs are for.

I have an app for that.

Jump Ropes

Along with the demise of spitballs came the tragic death of jump ropes. "A jump rope is very good exercise," someone told me. "They have them at the gym."

No, no, no. Jump ropes are for the sidewalk and they are supposed to be used for fun.

If you were a girl, what could be better than two friends, one rope, one afternoon and an endless list of nonsense verses of silly words that you could jump to?

> Teddy bear, teddy bear,
> Touch the ground.
> Teddy bear, teddy bear,
> Turn around.
> Teddy bear, teddy bear,
> Walk upstairs.

I got that from the internet, because I was a boy and there was no way I was going to learn jump rope songs.

If you were a boy, you were out of the picture. Don't ask why. Boys could not jump rope. Oh, sure, boxers would train with jump ropes, but they were sweaty and covered with muscles and they would never chant about a teddy bear.

Then the girls would use two ropes at one time, with one girl hopping over one and then the other so fast that no boy could figure out how she did it. The boys tried counting how fast the ropes twirled around.

One thousand one, "No, that's not fast enough."

It was a rope slapping the ground every half second. No, even that was not fast enough. So how did the girls do it?

We had no idea. So one boy would pull baseball or hockey cards out of his pocket.

"Anyone want to flip?"

Along with the tragic death of jump ropes came the disappearance of bubble gum cards.

You got them in a flat package with a flat piece of gum. The gum was bad for your teeth but the cards were wonderful for teaching you about gambling. The earlier you learned that you can lose everything, the better your life would be.

I once heard that the worst thing that can happen in betting on the horses is to win the first day you go to the track. I thought that was a dumb observation until I observed many people who won on their first bet. Hell. That is what it turned out to be.

From, "Look, I won. I won," to a few years later, "I have to win on this next horse or I will lose my house."

It happens. The only winner is the track, or the casino. It does not matter how many people tell you about their big wins, they do not tell you about the super-continuous big losses they have had on their way to the one big win, which pays back one fingernail of all the losses.

But I am not here to moralize, although I do a lot of that. Sorry.

I am here to be sad about the death of bubble gum cards that taught kids if they flip they will lose. Especially, they will lose the Mickey Mantle card that might someday be worth a fortune, if only it wasn't bent and twisted and had that sticky bit of gum that you sneaked onto it to cheat but it didn't work and the card stuck to the other cards after that and tore off part of Mickey's face.

If the cards were new and stiff you could stand back five or six steps from a wall and sail them like a Frisbee at the vertical obstruction. (I have no other way of saying that without repeating "Wall." Language is harder than flipping baseball cards.)

The closest one wins. Simple. But if you got a "leaner" you won. A "leaner" is with the card standing up against the wall. That makes you the winner unless the next card knocks down your "leaner" and falls on top of it. Then the card on top wins. That is, unless another card can be shown to be closer to the wall than the two cards that have just fallen down. Gambling has its rules.

It is sort of like watching Italians playing bocce. The rules change on every throw. "That ball is closer. Look, it is as close as my finger."

"It is as close as *my* finger and *my* finger is shorter than *your* finger."

Bocce is never boring, but don't bet on it.

Just as a side note, one of my favourite stories was in North Burnaby, about a bocce game being played by Italians right next to a lawn bowling game with English players.

There was a thin, non-soundproof wire fence separating the two games. On one side the Italians yelled and cheered and mumbled and applauded every throw.

On the other side the English folks smiled politely at a good throw and politely withheld negative comments at a bad toss. The most excited they got (on purpose, I have to add, because they did not want to look like their excited neighbours across the fence) was to clap for the winner of a match. But it was polite clapping, done with three fingertips softly stroking the palm of the other hand. No noise arose.

"This is very exciting," one of the English said quietly.

"Blankety, blank, blank blank," shouted one of the Italians on the other side of the fence when a ball was closer than his.

"They are quite outspoken," said the Englishman.

"We don't think they are having fun," said one of the Italians.

Of course they were. But it was contained fun.

Sorry. Back to baseball cards.

If the cards were too beaten up and wrinkled to fly, then you flipped them. You threw it down on the ground with a flip of the wrist. If you matched the previous face up or back of the card you won the card underneath yours. If not, you lost. If you missed landing on the card, the pile kept growing until someone could win the entire holdings of everyone else. Just like real life.

You sometimes thought you could control the way the cards landed, which turned out to be a lesson that paid off in gold when you lost. You did not get the gold, you just learned that your winning system has its drawbacks.

There are all sorts of people at the track and in casinos or in marriages who think they can control the future. It is a shame they didn't learn the lessons from flipping cards. If you went home with Mickey Mantle tonight, tomorrow night you could, and probably would, go home with nothing. And it was always tomorrow night.

There are still cards around, but they are in collections behind plastic sleeves and you cannot touch them. You do not flip them, you buy them and hope some other person who remembers childhood and has a lot of money will buy them from you. Again, a gamble.

And touching brings us to jacks. When the girls got tired of jumping ropes they got out their jacks, another tragic casualty of the electronic game.

Jacks were also amazing to boys because none of us could get our hands down on the ground fast enough to pick up the little pieces of metal between the bounces of the ball.

The metal jacks were like a cross with a third arm so that they stood up from the ground. But they were only a swipe up from scraping your fingertips on the concrete. When the boys tried it they banged their fingers on the sidewalk. The girls could bounce the small rubber ball, then scoop up half the jacks before the ball came down and they still could catch it in the hand that held the jacks. You try it. Your grandmother could do things you can't come close to.

The girls could do so many things the boys could not, like count and read and pick up jacks. And then there were marbles. That's a game like baseball cards, but with more history. I looked up the origin of marbles in a book about the history of all games and learned that marbles is simply the oldest game on earth. Egyptian kids played it while their parents were off building pyramids. Roman children played marbles while their parents were conquering the world.

Their marbles were usually small stones, not the neat glass balls with swirls of paint inside that we have now, but the basics were the same. Put some of your marbles down, draw a circle around them and see if someone else can knock them out of the circle.

That is too simple for most electronic games, but it kept kids going for 5,000 years, from 3,000 BC to 1980 when video games made their big push. I read that the games Egyptians played with the little round rocks were based on knocking one rock out of a circle in the sand.

Out of that game came golf, bowling, bocce, pool, field hockey and soccer. Probably others. That is not bad for a long-lasting bit of fun.

And I must mention that the best marble player I ever met was a girl. If you read an earlier book, the story is there, but she was simply the best. Dorothy, the girl who knew how to make hooks from safety pins when we went fishing in the sewers, also was one heck of a marble player.

The story in short, if you haven't read it, was that a kid from another neighbourhood was cleaning up everywhere he went. No one could beat him. His secret was a steel ball bearing. No glass marble on earth could knock that out of the ring.

He always pulled it out after he said, "No rules." That meant anything goes.

While Dorothy was kneeling next to the ring with the steel ball inside she got her biggest marble and pulled bubble gum from her mouth and wrapped it around her marble. Then she rolled it in the gravel until it was coated with tiny stones.

Then she fired it, and her rock-hard shot slammed into the ball of steel and did what no other marble had been able to do. She sent that shiny invader out of the ring, past the line and out into the world of losers.

We cheered. She had done the impossible and the nasty guy from far away got up and left with his bag of marbles, except it did not have his unbeatable iron ball banging around inside. He lost it to Dorothy.

You don't get that kind of battle with computer games.

But marbles are now, sadly, dead. The same with hopscotch, except I did see something about five years ago that made my heart glad.

A group of girls a block off Main Street made the longest hopscotch ever in the history of the world. It went on for four or five blocks. The only problem came when some boys tried to hop on it. But they didn't last long. Boys couldn't, and still can't, play hopscotch.

Now the games are mostly played alone with little hand-held pieces of plastic. The games are designed to make you want to buy the next game in the series. These are the games that are alive and thriving now. Along with the loss of the old games, that is truly tragic.

Pet Geranium

This is how a little kindness mixed with some craziness can possibly make you rich.

First of all almost everyone now wants a dog or a cat or a marmot, something warm and cozy to cuddle up with. Of course, when you feel that way you do not think of shots and neutering and picking up poop. And there is no thought of sifting kitty litter and sneezing and vacuuming hairs off the sofa.

But I have friends who solved all that. They had cats and dogs and fish. And after the pets had all died and were buried and the vet bills were paid off, they came upon a perfect companion.

A geranium.

"That's the most stupid idea since the pet rock," I told them, except the pet rock was not stupid at all because the people who thought of the pet rock made a fortune off it—but that was because no one had thought of it before and they sold tens of millions of them.

"No one makes money off stupid non-animal pet ideas anymore."

That is what I told my friends. But they said they did not care about making money, not at first anyway.

They got their pet geranium from a big shelf overloaded with geraniums. They felt sorry for it. It was at the end of the shelf and was getting ready to be knocked off.

It was one more life bred just to be a decoration. It would wind up in a pot for the summer, or put into the ground until winter came and then it would freeze to death. But there is another side to geraniums, they said, the friendly side.

Think of it as a furry little critter, the couple said. It is totally dependent on you. You have to bring it water or it will die. You have to give it light and turn it so it does not grow crooked. It is not like a pet rock, they said. It makes you feel needed without feeling silly. And, compared with animal pets, you feel needed without needing to get up at night. You can even scratch it behind its leaves.

This couple started taking their geranium out for walks. They made a little sling for it and carried it like a tiny bag of groceries. Later, as they grew closer, they started taking it on picnics, where it sat on the table. They even took it with them when they went shopping, but then they would leave it in the car.

"Certifiably nuts," I told them.

"Maybe, maybe not," they said.

Remember, there is nothing so good as a good idea. Other people started asking them about their geranium, a pet you can leave home for the weekend without feeling guilty.

And since everything becomes a fad, they said, we are just waiting. Just as soon as the right trendy people see it and it catches on, this will become a fad too. So my friends got to thinking. What every pet geranium will need is a little nameplate held up by a tiny chain, something to call their own. And maybe a little scarf to hang over their top branch, to make their nights comfy and cozy.

We all laughed at raincoats for dogs, remember? We said, "Who would buy a Sunday suit for Snuggles to wear while she walks the Seawall?" There are now at least three stores in Vancouver selling nothing but clothes for dogs.

My friends are now ready for the geranium revolution. They can order up the nameplates at a moment's notice and get scarf production rolling in a few days.

"Can you imagine the lineups?" my friend with the geranium said. "They will want nothing but the best for their little fuzzy sweethearts."

And if a year or so from now you are reading articles about pet geraniums being the biggest thing around, you will know it started with one little plant that was saved from being knocked off a shelf and forgotten in the shadows.

And if none of this happens, they still have their pet, which now has big flowers all over it.

"See," they said. "It likes us."

Another Harold Story

"I always try to leave extra time when I am going somewhere," said Harold.

There were three of us for coffee this morning: Harold, ninety-four; Don, eighty-one; and me, the baby at sixty-eight.

Originally there was just Harold and myself. We had two or three years of Tuesday morning coffee. Then we noticed a tall, thin guy sitting two tables away. After a few weeks we nodded. A few weeks later we said hello. A few weeks after that I asked his name. Don. The next week we asked if he would join us.

From then on it was Harold and Don and me. Don was a retired railroad cop, but that was a long time ago. He mostly listened to Harold's stories and filled in the gaps with growing-up stories of his own.

Now, back to Harold telling us he leaves extra time when going somewhere.

"For instance, this morning I wanted to put some flax seeds in the porch, but first I had to grind them up."

"Why are you using flax seeds?" I asked. "Are you feeding the birds?"

"They are good for digestion," he said.

"Of the birds?"

"What do birds have to do with it?" Harold asked.

"Isn't that why you are putting the seeds in the porch?"

Harold shook his head. How can anyone not understand something so simple, he thought. I know he thought that because he had made it clear what he was saying, he thought.

"No, not in the *porch*, in the porridge."

"I also thought you said porch," said Don.

It's so easy for anything we say not to be understood by someone or anyone we are talking with. If we only knew what was being heard when we were speaking we probably could get rid of divorce and wars and bad cooking.

"Why would I put the seeds in the porch? I don't even have a porch."

"So what does this have to do with having extra time?"

Harold smiled.

"I told you I had to grind up the seeds, and I have a coffee grinder. So I put the seeds in there."

He demonstrated with his hands. Hands were the first movies. He held the coffee grinder with his left hand and poured a scoop of seeds into the top.

"But it wouldn't work," said Harold. "There is a little slot in the grinder that the top fits into that makes it go, but the slot was jammed."

So he got out a knife. "It was a big knife, the one I use for carving roasts."

(Narratives, that means stories, are best when they keep going without interruptions in the action. But look at this sensibly. Why would a man who survived a war and the Depression and was a hobo and then a successful dentist use a knife with an eight-inch blade to poke the point into a slot smaller than his little toenail? Why do we buy a full-sized eight-cylinder 4,000-pound four-wheel drive to go to the hairdresser?)

"It was the only one I could reach," he said.

"I pushed the tip of the blade into the slot to clean it out."

But when he did, the grinder started. Of course it started. That is what the slot is for. That is what Harold had just told us. Push something into the slot and the slicing blades start spinning about 2,000 rpm. The slot is designed as a safety measure so that it will only start when the top is on.

"And there was no top on it," said Harold.

The seeds went flying and spraying and spinning and landed all over the counter, in the sink, on the floor and in Harold's hair and in his shirt pocket.

"I guess I should have thought of that," he said.

Well, yes.

And then he had to clean off the counter. Now Harold is a very bright guy. I have said this many times. I have marvelled at the astronomy magazines he brings to our coffee meetings and the discussions we have about splitting the atom and I have listened with admiration and personal mind mush when he tells me about the periodic table of elements. But failing to put the top on a grinder before grinding? Duh.

"I tried to sweep up the seeds, but the plug was still in the wall and the cord would only let me get the grinder near to the edge of the counter but not past the counter."

That was not far enough to actually sweep the seeds into the open grinder.

"Why didn't you unplug it?"

"Because I wanted to grind them. So I tried to sweep them up and throw them into the grinder."

That meant trying to scoop the seeds up and move them several inches through the air. That, of course, was contrary to the laws of physics and gravity, which Harold has studied for decades.

"So the seeds wound up on the floor."

"Did you get any in your porridge?"

"Of course. I picked them off the counter and put a handful in the pot."

"And the seeds on the floor?"

"I'll clean them up when I get home unless the mice get to them."

"Do you have mice?"

"No, but the seeds on the floor might attract them."

"And then what?"

"I'll put out some traps."

"Why didn't you clean them up before you left?"

"I didn't put aside that much time and I wanted to be on time for coffee."

As a species we excel at contradictions.

"But I still thought he said *porch*," Don whispered to me.

"Me too," I whispered back.

And then Don was not there the following week, nor two weeks later. He never came back. Of course he might have been away, or sick, or anything.

But he was not there. I have no way of knowing what happened. But, Don, whatever happened to you, and wherever you are, you were right. Harold said "porch." He said it clear as a bell, not "porridge."

It is good to know you were right, no matter where you are.

P.S. Two months later:

This morning, the morning of the day I am to send this manuscript to the publisher, I was having coffee with Harold when Don came walking into the coffee shop.

"Where have you been? I thought you were dead."

"Tuesday mornings did not fit in with my schedule," he said. "I had friends to meet at another coffee shop."

That is amazing. No, not that he has other places and friends, but that an eighty-one-year-old has a schedule. If you are twenty-five you think you are the only one with things to do and places to be, but that never changes.

When you are eighty-one, or ninety-four, you will still have an appointment calendar, at least in your head. Older folks are like younger folks, only smart enough to order coffee with less sugar.

And as I said this morning, "You were right, Don. Harold said porch." I'm glad you got to hear that.

David and Goliath

What we need are characters. We need individuals who do something and stand up for something and stir up the works.

Occasionally they come along and the newspapers and television stations love them and then the population loves them and then they are gone, and we are sad.

One was David Alexander. He was one of the best. I just came back from writing his obituary.

This story is nothing but praise for a strange fellow with a long beard who went shirtless in the summer and stopped traffic on the Lougheed Highway and made the world a better place. Of course, if you were in civic government in Maple Ridge in the late 1990s you would have hated him.

He was a disgrace, an embarrassment and a traffic hazard and anything else that you could think of. The mayor and council wanted him out because, well, because he was there where everyone could see him.

If you don't know his story, imagine a shanty town on the side of the highway between Maple Ridge and Mission. It started with a few items for sale, like a garage sale, off to the side of the road. Dave got tables and chairs and old saws and dolls and put them up for viewing at a small pull-off.

Then he got more. And more. And he put them up for sale. Then he built a shack to keep out of the rain and he filled the shack with more stuff, so he put an extension on the shack and filled that.

This was in the late 1970s, when hippies were mainstream and men with beards doing odd things were not so odd. He put up a sign on his shack that said: *Dave's World*. And he got more stuff. He got it from the recycling depot and from junkyards and from any place that had anything. He didn't pay for any of his things.

Cars began to stop and folks wandered around his things. Sometimes the folks bought things, like I bought one rusty, four-wheeled roller skate with wheels that would not turn.

What the heck did you get that for? That was my wife asking. She was not happy with my purchase, even though it was only a dollar.

I got it because it reminded me of the time when I was a kid and we made scooters out of skates and wooden boxes and two-by-fours. They would last only a few hours, but in that time we had the best times of our lives, until we made something else.

That skate sat on my desk for more than a year before I was finally talked into getting rid of it. It was replaced by a plastic rendition of Oscar the Grouch coming out of a garbage can. You can read about him somewhere else in this book. Both Oscar and the roller skate are keys to entering a good time in life.

That is what Dave gave to thousands. One by one they stopped, and sometimes five or ten or more, and that became a bit of a traffic problem, but that is part of life—unless you happen to be the police who do not like parts of life that operate outside of the rules and report the problem to city hall and say *something* must be done about this.

You cannot blame the police—that's their job—but you can blame the politicians who cannot see potential beyond the rules.

And then Dave got more stuff. By the time city hall was steaming angry he had taken over about twenty car-lengths of the side of the highway. Many said it was a tourist attraction. Many said it was better than anything in Maple Ridge. Many made Dave's World part of their weekend outing.

And others said Dave had to go.

City hall passed new rules or decided to enforce old rules, it does not matter which. When a force gets into motion it is unimportant how it gets going. It just goes. Doing it is what counts, and city hall was doing it, with gritted teeth and adamant statements.

The mayor of the time is still on tape saying Dave must go. No, I can't describe it here. On tape it looks fierce. Dave *must go*. He is violating rule number something and ordinance number something else.

The city came to haul his stuff away. That was not nice, because it was his stuff, but they started throwing it into dumpsters and Dave did the same thing most people would do. He fought back and said don't take my stuff.

And then there was a scuffle and the police tackled Dave and handcuffed him and charged him with resisting arrest. It often happens that way unless you are a banker charged with defrauding thousands of people of millions of dollars. Then there is no tackling, the wrists are cuffed gently and there are no extra charges. Big-time criminals are always aware of their image.

Two years later the charges against Dave were dismissed. That is speedy justice. And then he ran for mayor and got 3,000 votes, which was not quite enough but it shocked a lot of people who did not vote for him as well as many who did. He had a great deal of support.

And that means there were many people who thought Dave's

World was a good thing and Dave with a white beard that went down to his chest and an eclectic fascination with rusty roller skates and politics was not a bad guy.

He passed away in his trailer in Mission in June 2012. No one knows exactly when he died. He was alone. He was found dead. It could have been the day before or several days before. He was sixty-five.

The pull-off in the road at 272 Street is now overgrown with weeds. You could not tell it from any other pull-off anywhere along the road. I had trouble finding it when I went back after I learned he died. But it is not just that nothing is there. The sad part is, something is missing. Pity. For us.

Keep Blowing Your Horn

"I'm going to wait 'til midnight and blow my horn out the window, if I'm still awake," said Harold.

He was sitting across from me in a coffee shop on our weekly Tuesday morning visit, and I had asked what he was going to do for New Year's Eve.

But he didn't really want to talk about horns or New Year's Eve. That was not a challenge. Anyone can blow a horn out a window. He said he wanted to exercise his mind, so he was memorizing the Lord's Prayer.

"Oh, come on, Harold," I said. "That's like saying you want to exercise your arms and you pick up one-pound dumbbells."

"It's good for me," he said.

"Everyone already knows it," I said. "Especially you."

Harold's parents were missionaries in India in the very early 1900s. Harold was born in India. He went to a Christian church run by his parents for the first nine years of his life. He played around a Christian hospital operated by his parents. The Lord's Prayer was everywhere.

"I never listened to it," he said.

He is, and he says he always has been, an atheist.

"The creation of the universe was a giant explosion, which still happens in smaller ways with supernovas," he said. He has said this numerous times to me.

Then, in Tim Hortons, with a window painting of Frosty the Snowman behind him, Harold started talking about his favourite subject: nuclear power. He talked of the giant cyclotron in Switzerland where atoms are driven up to nearly the speed of light and then smashed into each other in a true headbanger of a crash.

"And there are things that escape from the nucleus and no one knows what they are," he said with a beaming face. "Some call it dark matter. That is the glue that holds everything together. That is called the Higgs-boson effect."

Then he described who Mr. Higgs was, including his fat, round belly. Then he talked of how many protons there are in an oxygen atom, "And it is the same everywhere in the universe."

His eyes were wide. He did not want to stop talking. He drew $E=mc^2$ on a napkin and started explaining how matter can turn into energy and energy into matter.

People at the next table were talking about the weather.

Then he asked if I thought nuclear power would ever become popular. No, I said. Not for a long, long time, because many fear it like the witches of the Middle Ages. They could do anything with their boiling pots and spells and bats' wings, but in the end they would hurt you. The same with nuclear power.

He looked sad, but agreed. I slid my hand over the table and picked up the napkin with the $E=mc^2$ on it and put it in my pocket. It would be a memory.

Harold had his ninety-fourth birthday three days before Christmas. He came to our home for a party. He drove there. When he was eighty-nine he rode his motorcycle to our house for tea.

"Tell me more about the horn you are going to blow on New Year's."

You have to ask questions. Questions are good. It is better to ask someone about themselves than to say, "I do that too. I know that. I have a horn. I like horn music. I once played a horn in a band. I, me, horn. Me. Me. Me. I. I. I."

When you talk about yourself you kill the conversation.

"It used to have a rubber bulb at the end. You squeezed it and it blew. But that rotted away long ago. So now I hold it to my mouth and blow."

This is no ordinary horn. Where did it come from? I asked.

"My father's car in India."

Oh, lord. His father went to India in 1915. Harold had told me his father had one of the few cars ever seen there at the time. He had an Indian driver so he could treat medical emergencies far from the hospital and so the family could treat itself to a luxury befitting their status.

The horn was on the side of the car.

"It has hung on my wall for thirty or forty years."

From what I know about his past, that was about the time of his divorce.

"I have to clean it once in a while with Salvo."

The story was going to end there, and I was going to tell you that on New Year's Eve Harold blew his horn, maybe for the last time, maybe not. That is a good ending for a story.

But as we left the coffee shop he said he had gotten a phone call several days earlier from someone from his bank who seemed to know a great deal about his account, but he wanted more information.

Nooo, I said. Noooooo, I thought. Don't give any information over the phone. No. Please, say you didn't.

"I felt so embarrassed afterwards. I know I shouldn't have, but he seemed to want to transfer some of my money to GICs."

Nooooo. Not by phone, I thought.

He was driving right up to the bank to talk to them.

"I hope you're okay," I said. I prayed he had not been swindled out of his money.

Later that day he called.

"You can't guess what happened," he said.

He drove into the underground parking lot. His was the only car.

He got his walker off the hooks on the back of the car and went to the elevator. He got in and rode to the main floor and got out.

"Hello," he said.

No answer. There was no one in the bank.

He could see other people on the outside of the glass door using the automated tellers. They saw him and tried the doors to get in.

Locked.

"Hello?"

No answer.

In a few minutes a young Mountie rushed up to the doors.

"Mufffle, muffin, dooooing, there?!!??"

"I don't understand you," said Harold.

"*Waaaadyoudoointherrrrr?*" the young Mountie repeated very loudly.

"I still don't understand you," said Harold, who was sitting on the seat of his walker.

Then there were two more Mounties outside the glass door repeating what the first Mountie had said.

Harold pointed to his ears and shook his head.

"Then I thought it was time to get out of there before I got into trouble," he told me.

He got his walker back to the elevator, pushed the button, the door opened and he rode down to the parking lot.

"There was a reception committee down there," he said.

The police surrounded him and asked how much cash he had.

"None," he said. "That's why I went to the bank."

They wanted to know how he got into the bank. He told them. Then they wanted to know again. He told them again. Then they asked him to explain how he got into the bank.

They looked at his driver's licence and asked how he got into the bank.

Eventually they let him go.

"I'm glad they didn't handcuff me and take me to the police station. It's hard to walk with a walker while in handcuffs."

The next day he called the bank. His money was safe and the nice man on the phone told him that the computer locking system was not set for a holiday on Tuesday when Christmas is Sunday. It was probably programmed by an American company that does not celebrate Boxing Day.

Four days later at midnight Harold's horn was silent and he was sleeping. He had had a busy week.

She Looked Beautiful

(This was written six months before any politics came into the story. This is not an endorsement of a candidate. It is simply an endorsement of life, which beats politics any time.)

She looked wonderful. She looked radiant. Okay, she looked beautiful, glowing, although that might get me in trouble with my wife.

I was inside a meeting room at the Dr. Sun Yat-sen Classical Chinese Garden last weekend when the government was announcing that both Chinatown and the garden would be made national historical sites.

For this I was glad. Chinatown has more history than any other part of this city. If it were not for the spices and sweat of the Chinese, this city would be only a half-baked English village with bad food.

Look at all the businesses, engineers and bankers, not to mention the restaurants and the lonely labourers who built the railroads. But this is not about the Chinese. It is about a woman who is part black and part white, and is beautiful.

She was not always so. The last pictures of her in the newspaper more than three years ago showed a haggard, tired woman who had been arrested for drunk driving. She had a problem. Lots of us have that problem.

You take one drink, then you take another. It feels so good. Then you take another. And another. In time you look haggard. And you can't drive very well, even though you think you can, so you get behind the wheel and drive, and others say, "Look at that drunk weaving across the road."

If you get lucky you get arrested before you hit someone.

I have done so many stories on the good folks of Skid Row who have broken their addictions to drugs and alcohol. They are uplifting because you know all they have gone through; poverty, crime, sometimes hunger, and almost always brutality.

And there are others who give up their lives to stuff they inhale or inject or drink. They are your neighbours. They are the ones you have coffee with at work. They have homes and cars and children and responsibilities. They, in some cases, are you.

You know who you are. You try to live a life with a paycheque and movies with your spouse and even church, occasionally. But then you sneak down to the basement or into the kitchen cabinet when you get a moment alone and grab the bottle. You don't pour a glass, you just unscrew the top and tilt it back. Then you do it again, because you might not be able to get to the bottle again for ten or fifteen minutes. Then you do it again.

Then you open the refrigerator and swallow some milk to cover the smell. And you are in your forties or fifties or sixties. And you are doing what you would ridicule and despise if you heard someone else you knew was doing it.

And then you go back for another swallow. Quick. Someone is coming.

And you feel good, until you get drowsy and it is only 8 p.m., and you talk but the words don't sound right. Still, you can fool anyone. You just won't talk. You can get away with it.

Then your spouse or kids ask if you are feeling all right and you try to say you are a little tired and you fall down on the bed and that's it for the night.

And you are fine all the next day, and you say you won't do that again. Then comes the night and you head like a robot to the hiding place and you are alone and you grab the bottle and unscrew the top.

Constance Barnes had some of that going on. I don't know what the tricks were, but they were there. The extra problem she had was she was a politician. At that time she was a member of the Park Board, so when she was arrested she was in the newspaper. And she did not look pretty.

But that was three years ago, maybe more.

Now I looked at Constance Barnes, who is now the head of the Park Board of which the Sun Yat-sen Garden is a part, working in the background while the Chinese community leaders and the government people got the spotlight.

But when I saw her smiling at the rear of the crowd it looked like some personal light was on her alone.

I said, "You look super good."

She said simply, "Sobriety is wonderful."

That was all. That was all she had to say. It was much better than a big government announcement about a garden and a neighbourhood being proclaimed a historic site.

History, no matter how fascinating, is obviously about the past. And often that is ugly and hard. What Constance Barnes said is about the future. And the future looked beautiful.

Let's Have a Celebration of the Outdoors, as Planned by the Government

As I say, I saw Constance Barnes at the press conference about the garden. She had nothing to do with setting it up. She was there as a representative of the Park Board. The setting up part was done from on high.

Occasionally the federal government, which is in Ottawa, makes a move that does not upset anyone. It makes the government feel loved when it doesn't get yelled at.

The government declared the Sun Yat-sen Garden in Vancouver's Chinatown a national moment.

"We will now announce this to the country," said someone in the government.

"We should do it at the garden," said a brilliant subordinate.

They invited dignitaries from the Chinese community and dignitaries from the government and dignitaries from other dignified places to a press conference in the place of honour.

Some of the dignitaries were flown in from Ottawa.

From the airport and other places they were brought to the garden by special buses and limousines with darkened windows because dignitaries should see but not be seen. And they were ushered into the garden through a beautiful entrance lined with beautiful carvings.

They did not have time to look at the carvings because they were led down a covered hallway into a meeting room. Inside were rows of chairs and there was a podium at the front. There is a roof on this room and there are walls. There are windows on one side, but the dignitaries had many support staff who did not have chairs to sit on so they stood around the walls, including in front of the windows.

Television cameras were lined up in front of the podium where the dignitaries would speak.

The meeting began with speeches. Then there were more speeches. Each speaker read from papers that had words that described the beauty of the garden. They said it was a classic jewel in the city.

The press conference was scheduled to last an hour, which is a very long time to listen to speeches, so I went outside and met an old Chinese man walking alone by the pond.

Hello. The usual greetings.

"Why are they in there?" he asked.

"Because this is an important place and they want to talk about it."

"But the important place is out here," he said.

His name is Julian Law. He was ninety-three when I met him. He is a volunteer who comes to the garden every day to tell visitors about it.

"You see this stone?"

He put his foot on a large rock that looked sort of like a turtle.

"It is a tortoise. They are not in a hurry and they live a long time."

"You see those curved edges at the bottom of the roofs?"

I saw. I nodded.

"They catch bad spirits that may fall from the sky and they throw them back up away from the garden."

I felt relieved and safe.

"You see the holes in the rocks?"

Most of the large rocks that were brought from China for the garden have softly smooth holes.

"They are for the good spirits to live in."

I felt I was in good company.

I said I had to go back inside and check on the dignitaries.

They were still speaking. One speaker reading from a paper on the podium said the garden was made of trees and shrubs and rocks that have ancient Chinese spiritual meanings. There was a light on the speaker for the cameras.

I asked one of the support staff, who was from Ottawa and was standing at the back of the room, why this was not being held outside.

"It always rains in Vancouver," he said.

"But it's not raining," I said.

"We couldn't take the chance. And if it got windy there would be no way to keep the papers on the podium."

The podium had been flown in from Ottawa.

I went outside again and found Julian smiling.

"You feel the breeze?" he asked. "Chinese believe that it is a kiss on the cheek and it brings good luck."

I was glad to be kissed.

Then the press conference ended and I went back to the room to see what would happen. And what do you think happened?

You are right.

The dignitaries left. Their support staff packed up the papers and the podium and walked out of the room, through the hallway and out the door.

"Are you going to tour the garden?" I asked one young woman from Ottawa.

"No time," she said. "A tight schedule."

And poof. The buses and limos pulled away and disappeared.

I went back to Julian.

"You know that tortoise rock you showed me?"

He nodded.

"He is very smart," I said.

Hosing Away the Garbage

You have almost no education. You have no teeth in the front. You have a family. That is simply, well, I want to say "dumb," but you're not alone.

It looks like you can't get a job. It looks like you can't support your family. So why did you have a family? Why didn't you get more education? (The teeth are your own decision and I have no right to ask.)

And besides that, where else did you go wrong?

Everywhere. You know that. You have crashed through all the rungs on the ladder of success. Like so many, you started at the bottom and then went down, and your offspring don't so much spring as fall. Blame your ancestors.

Ancestors? Are you kidding? Ancestors are for the rich. You know nothing about them.

Well, think of your descendants!

Are you kidding? They will happen because we at this end of the scale seem to be more fertile (that's a fancy word that I don't usually use) than folks at the other end. In fact folks at the other end spend big money if they are *not* fertile. They *want* a baby. At this end, we really *don't* want another baby, but they come along anyway. And there is no chance for them.

Not a good resumé.

His name? Greg Wells. Needs a shave. Needs bridge work in front. Doesn't need any more children—he already has four.

He enters the Personnel Department of a business, any business, anywhere.

"Experience?"

"I work hard."

"But what do you do?"

"Anything."

"Are you computer literate?"

"Can't afford one."

"Sorry, Mr. ... what was your name? I'm afraid we don't have any openings just now."

Just now?

"That happened, and happened, and, well, you know."

Greg Wells was talking to me near the garbage transfer station off Southwest Marine Drive. Except for the stink of the garbage it would be an idyllic spot, a very short walk to the Fraser River, which was flowing long before Simon Fraser's name was put on it. It had many fish then. Now finding a fish is like finding a job.

"So I thought, what can I do that they can't do?" said Greg.

"I can stand the stink."

This is not what someone with long, tapered fingers that touch the key pad of a hand-sized computer would think. Thank goodness.

"Would you like this truck washed?" Greg asked a supervisor at the transfer station that transfers our garbage to some other place that we don't know about.

The truck was coated with goop and glob and banana peels and rotting meat and plastic bags filled with things that good citizens pick up when they walk their dogs. You don't want to go there.

The short of that conversation was that the supervisor actually needed, somehow, to get the trucks at least clean enough to pass along a city street but he had no one who would do it. It was not in any government contract.

Greg cleaned one truck. Then another one.

The next day he brought two of his sons.

They cleaned all the trucks.

This is not like washing a car. This is using a fire hose and pounding on the cemented garbage that started in your kitchen and then went to the curb and then went into a garbage truck and then to a transfer station in North Vancouver or Burnaby or Richmond and then got transferred again to a spot near the idyllic Fraser River and then got scooped into a truck that carries twenty tons (don't worry if that is metric or standard—it is huge and it stinks) and then got hauled to "Cash" Creek to a hole in the ground where your pet's poo will rest for a thousand years.

When the big trucks come back they look like they are returning from D-Day. I don't mean to disrespect D-Day—that was truly the holiest day of the modern era—but there is no better image. The trucks are beaten and covered with things you don't want to know about.

"I'll clean them," said Greg.

In the ten years he has been doing this he has made a good living for his family. His sons are soon to take over the business. They pull out a fire hose and scour the sides of the trucks, and one of them ("It's your turn." "No, it's yours.") has to go underneath the truck with the nozzle of the hose and beat away at stuff that has seeped through.

"I hate that job," said Ben Wells, Greg's son. "But it is better than not working and my father has given me this and I'm not letting go."

152

And then there was a picture. You need a picture to understand this.

One long-haul truck, about twenty feet high, or the height of three and a half large men, pulled up and parked. There was a background of a mountain of garbage and then three brooms started scrubbing the side of the truck. One father and two sons were making a living. No one asked for their resumés.

The rest of us need the internet. They don't.

"I could send my sons anywhere and they would outwork any man," said Greg.

He is the ancestor. His kids are the descendants.

Lucky descendants.

The Future

I never write or think about fiction. How could I? With a life such as we have around us, who could make up something better?

But there is the future. And when you look around you can see that what is coming is incredible, and not fiction at all.

Throughout our history, all stories, and I mean *all* stories, began with Once Upon A Time. Those stories were told when the past was the only thing we could think of as having a magic to it. It was the past of so long ago that no one remembered it. It was so far back in the folds of time that no one could say it was not so. It was once upon a time.

We are different, and that is because of the computer. Suddenly our lives have changed. We look down at a piece of plastic in our hands to communicate. We type messages that tell someone we are having coffee. We have a question and we look up the answer on the thing in our hands. And this is just the beginning.

IBM, International Business Machines for you who don't know

it started off as a maker of cash registers, has invented, or discovered, a memory storage sort of thing (there is no other word for it but a *thing*) that is twelve atoms big, or small.

Twelve atoms!!!!! That is smaller than a breadbox, and no one alive knows how big a breadbox is. Twelve atoms is impossible. The folks at IBM had to use a super-powerful electronic microscope just to see it, much less invent it.

But this thing that is smaller than a sniff of air (in fact a sniff of air has billions of atoms), this *thing* has a memory that can hold Ones and Zeros, which are the basics of computer thought. It doesn't matter that it can only hold a few odd thoughts; it doesn't matter that it has to be at absolute zero to do it (absolute zero, as you know, is −273°C). The folks at IBM say that to make a storage container that can hold memory at room temperature they have to put together 150 atoms! My heavens. That is something caught on the back of a hair in my nose that I never felt!

Their only problem is they don't know how to package this thing. If it came as a Christmas present it could fit in the dirt under your fingernail even after you've had a manicure.

The point is, the future will be different. The entire history of the world could very soon be put on a chip smaller than small.

There will be no point in libraries or museums or newspapers or grocery lists. There will still be librarians looking for things on the chip, but no need for shelves with books. And there will be museum curators who will tell you where to go on the chip to find pictures of dinosaurs, but no need to put together their bones. Even now people check their smart phone to see if they need beans, but soon the refrigerator will make the list for you and it will be forwarded to the delivery service. Gone will be the art of forgetting the turnips because you don't like turnips.

I have thought about this, and what I'm going to tell you is possibly not fiction.

Once Upon A Long Time From Now, this happened.

A monk was living a simple life in a remote monastery.

He had been taught that the god they all believed in had created the earth and the heavens and everything in seven days, and not very long ago.

He, and everyone else, knew this because their data bank had the information stored in it.

The earth was barren, but nothing needed to grow because the sun gave the inhabitants all their energy.

The monk (his name was Darwin) rolled around on his wheels and got his food and all his earthly needs through the solar panel that was on his head.

"The sun gives us everything, and it is a gift," they said in prayer.

And then Darwin and the other monks studied the history of everything that told them that everything was created in a week and they were the last things that were created and everyone was happy.

But one day old Darwin was rolling around the wide, desolate fields and came upon a pile of stuff. He had never seen this stuff before.

The stuff was behind a fence that had fallen down and on the fence was a sign that said Junk Yard, but Darwin did not know what that meant.

He dug around in the pile and found something that was straight and made of metal and had a flat point at one end and a round grip at the other. It made no sense to him, but we know he had found a screwdriver.

Then he dug around some more and found something that had two straight pieces of metal that were connected in the centre with a kind of bolt. This, also, made no sense to him, but we know he had found a pair of pliers.

He brought them back to the monastery and put them under his bed, and before he plugged in his battery for the night he said to himself, "This stuff is strange."

He was not a deep thinker.

A while later, after many more mornings with the other monks who said together that the earth was created in seven days, he went out to the pile again.

Darwin dug around and found a box made of plastic, just like him, but it had wires sticking out of it, unlike him, and dials, unlike him, and a cone that crumbled when he touched it. Whoops. Don't touch.

We know he had found a radio.

The next day, while the monks were talking about everything being made in seven days, he wondered when these things that he had found had come about.

Later he went out to the pile and found something sort of like the box with a cone, but it had a front made of glass, and then he found a very heavy hunk of metal with big holes in it and things that apparently went up and down inside the holes.

We know he had found a television and an internal combustion engine.

Many more days went by with mornings spent talking about the seven days and afternoons spent at the pile, where he found things that had apparently grown into other things.

"We know everything there is to know," said the chief monk. "We have been given this knowledge from the beginning and we were created in seven days. That is that and that is all that there is."

And then Charles (that is what his friends called him) went out to the pile and found another piece of plastic that had a screen and buttons but not much else. It looked a little like him, but a very crude him.

You know what he had found—a laptop.

After several more visits he came upon a BlackBerry and an iPhone, and Darwin said, "These are from a long time ago, longer ago than the seven days."

He went back to the monastery and told the other monks what he had found and what he thought.

"Be careful, Charlie, or you will have the black cloth pulled over your head," they said.

"But look," said Charles, and he took out of his carrying box some cell phones and iPhones and other pieces of what he said looked like an earlier life.

"Get them out of here," said the other monks. "Those are a blasphemy. Those are untruths."

But Darwin continued to go to the pile until eventually the chief monk called him to a meeting and said, "I have heard about what you are bringing into the minds of the other monks. You must stop."

"But it is true," said Darwin. "There was something before us. I have the proof."

The chief monk said, "I will give you two choices. Either you forget about whatever fantasy and falsehood you say you have found, or you will have the black cloth pulled over your head."

Darwin had one day to think about it. He went back to the pile.

"But it is true," he said.

The next day, before the black cloth was put on his head, he said to the chief monk and the other monks, "There was something that came before us. Whatever it was started with one cell and then became two, and eventually evolved into us."

"Give me the black cloth," said the chief monk. And he pulled it over Charlie's solar panel.

Just before Darwin's system fizzled, he said from under the cloth, "But it is true."

The only thing he didn't know, and no one ever knew, was who made the screwdriver.

THE END, until it is a news story.

And Now Today

May 2, 2012, not far in the past.

I was sitting in an edit room at the television station working on a simple story. A girl had beaten all the boys in ringing the bell at Playland.

She had taken a plastic-covered sledge hammer and hit a cone hard enough to ring the bell. Of course it is now all done electronically. You don't see a piece of metal flying up a giant thermometer-like scale until it hits the bell. But it's still pretty good.

She weighed about one hundred pounds and swung that ten-pound hammer like a champ. Bang.

I felt wonderful. Just seeing her doing the big swing was good enough for me, but then I saw several boys take turns after her and fail to ring the bell. I felt better than wonderful. Girl beats boys. Wonderful.

This was especially great because we had just left Cambie Street after a strikeout, which means a failure in any language. On the median on Cambie Street, a wide field of grass between the lanes of traffic, a young lady was picking mushrooms. That made me feel good, until she said she didn't want to be on television.

Darn. Look at those mushrooms. Look at you. Look at the subway below it, which we cannot actually see, but since the street was dug up, the tunnel was put in below and the street was replaced, the pristine grass now has mushrooms growing in it. This was a chance to see how the world has changed, but we can't do it without the girl picking mushrooms.

You know the rules. The story must almost always have someone in it or it becomes an essay, and you cannot overdo essays or you will look like you are trying to be Andy Rooney and I am just a humble reporter, not a commentator, unless I can sneak in the commentary over pictures of a person doing something.

But she doesn't want to be photographed, so I go away.

And a half-hour later I see the girl with the hammer. Thank you.

The story is fine. It is done quickly. I am out of there and heading for the newsroom.

Everything so far is the way it goes in human experience. Success, failure, success. We can deal with that.

In the newsroom, 1 p.m., the editor puts down some of the pictures and I write: "This is what we hoped to see. Look at her, looking up at the bell, because the bell is ringing and she is a *she!*"

That is television writing. It would fail in an English class, but it is real and it is human and we understand it, and then ... the screen went dark.

Whoops. Darn. Several others in the dark hallway of the editing world said the same thing. Darn. And worse.

The picture of the girl froze on the high-definition screen in front of us.

The editor, Chris Koster, pushed some buttons and said something like darn. Chris knows which buttons to push. He is a magician with magical computer buttons. Then the picture jumped and came back to life and everything returned to normal. Chris shrugged. He didn't know what had gone wrong or how it got fixed.

I picked up the microphone.

Zing. Or maybe it was zap.

The picture froze again. Bad words came from down the hallway. Other moving pictures had turned to ice. All the edit rooms in the station had frozen. Engineers came in like the marines, swarming over the keyboards. They typed but nothing happened. They worried and nothing happened.

Then suddenly, on the screen, the girl's hammer continued down and hit the cone and the bell rang.

Okay, everything would be good ... again.

As soon as the engineers left, the picture froze ... again. If this is mind-numbing to read, it was much worse to be there. But the show had to go on, and other human brains in other newsrooms were putting it together. Stories were edited in the remote satellite and microwave trucks. Reporters in the television station went on the set live and read their stories. A satellite feed from a traffic helicopter in Seattle showing a protest similar to the one in Vancouver was put on the air.

In short, the producers magically made a newscast out of thin air. They should have been congratulated. In fact, they *were* congratulated. The next day the news director said they were wonderful and the chief of all the computer wizards explained what happened.

"Brain split."

The invisible lightning-firing electrons in the computer brain had created a traffic jam.

In short, the main program had gone down, a human word meaning it crashed. But the backup program was there, as planned, and it could handle everything, the programmers said.

So everything shifted to the backup program. Then the main program came back to life. That happens in religions, politics and computers. Everything shifted back to the main program ... and then it went down for the second time.

Shift again. Then it came back. Shift. Then it went down. Shift. It came back and then went down, again.

At that moment, the person in charge of everything in the computer world explained, "The edit rooms voted on which program they would join."

The editors did not vote. The human people who do the editing did not vote. The rooms voted, or rather the computer terminals in each room cast a ballot. No humans were bribed in the process.

And the vote? It was a tie.

What happens in life when there is a tied vote? Nothing. We have another vote, but the computer terminals are not into overtime voting so, to put it simply, nothing happened. And the news show was saved by human thinking and sweaty palms.

But just think, the individual computer terminals voted, without any human intervention. They are programmed to do this, and someday they will be programmed to make a decision on what to do if they don't know what to do, which is something that we as humans do. Now go back and reread the previous story—especially the last sentence.

The Culprit

I had a conversation with the Earth. It was friendly at first. It began with, "Hello."

I was in a park and I sat down on a concrete bench on an asphalt walkway just off a busy street. It was a typical park in a typical city.

"You talking to me?" said the Earth.

"Well, yes. Isn't that you with the grass and the tree and the sign that says 'Keep Off'?"

"This is me," said the Earth. "But if you want to commune with Nature you've got to come closer."

"Can't you hear me from here?" I asked. "I just want to tell you how lucky you are because the environment is *in*.

"What does that mean?" asked the Earth.

I was happy. I could tell the Whole Earth how blessed it was to have us crawling around on its skin, because when something is

Fashionable, when something is In Style, there is nothing we will not do to make everyone fall in line.

"It means you are now Numero Uno. We all Love you. We have big campaigns saying, 'Love The Earth or Die.'"

Actually we do not have those campaigns yet but if the temperature gets any hotter we will.

"If you love me why are you killing me?" asked the Earth.

"Are you crazy?" I asked, but the Earth did not hear me because some kids on skateboards went by. They had earplugs attached to music boxes in the sides of their heads but their music was so loud it drowned out what I was saying.

I knew as the kids grew more and more deaf they would turn up their music even louder. This hurt, because I was going to mention how we are helping nature by creating parks where people could go and listen to the birds.

"You can't hear my birds any more with that racket," said the Earth. "In fact the only birds that can live in your cities are pigeons, and even I think they are not the brightest things alive."

Overhead, a jetliner was passing by making a long, anorexic vapour cloud behind it. I could see about six clouds like that. We were not too far from an airport. If all those Twiggie clouds got together they would make a Tubby.

"That ticks me off," said the Earth. "The fumes from cars get stuck under those clouds. It's hard for me to get a deep breath."

"We're switching to electric cars," I said. "We care about you."

"It took you long enough. But then you will build more dams to make more electricity and even now there are not many places for my fish to snuggle up. And no snuggle, you know, means no fish."

"We breed them on farms," I said. "We have taken the work out of fish creation. Again, we are just trying to help you."

"But you catch all the little fish to feed to the farm fish and that leaves no little fish for my big fish to eat. And that means the whales that you are no longer killing you are now starving to death."

I thought the Earth was getting a little testy. We take good care of our whales in tanks in aquariums. What more do you want? Only I didn't say that because an angry Earth could open up and swallow me. I saw that in a movie once and, even though I know it was done on a computer, you can't be too careful.

"We have laws that people now have to pick up after their dogs," I said.

"And you know what the dogs think of that?" said the Earth. "I happen to know because they are part of Nature and I am all of Nature and I know everything that happens in Nature including what dogs think."

"What do dogs think?"

"They think humans have a strange attraction to poop, especially dog poop. They want to get rid of it and they see you all gathering it and taking it home. They think you are strange. Sometimes they think it is hard to live with you."

"But we are just trying to keep *you* clean."

"Poop never bothered me, but I think you are more worried about your shoes than my shoulders. And while we are talking about cleaning up, there is something else I wish you would clean up."

"What?" I started to ask, when my hand-held computer began to play Mozart's Violin Concerto no. 5 in A Major. I not only get messages, I get culture.

I ignored my conversation with the Earth and pushed a button on a device that was once a telephone but can now do everything the rocket-launching computers could do twenty years ago. In fact it can do more. The rocket-launching computers could not Tweet or Facebook or find me a restaurant. But most of all, the giant computers could not fit in my pocket and ache to be held every five minutes.

"That is what I want to talk to you about," said the Earth.

I held my finger over my lips to shush up the Earth. Did it not know I was getting a Text? Did it not know a text is more urgent than dirt and grass or even a human being standing next to you? Where have you been, Earth?

Anyway, my text was from a friend to all his friends saying he had a new app that organizes his apps and now life would be simple.

"I would like to say ...," said the Earth.

"Just a second," I said, and now I was just a little annoyed. "Text messages *have* to be answered immediately or the sender will think you are not there."

"You look like Zombies," said Earth. "You cross the street looking down at your hand. You walk your dog looking down at your hand. You make love, then stop to read a text. You have gone crazy."

I did not hear the Earth. I was texting.

"Did you know that the fast food places are now posting signs saying how many calories are in their burgers?"

I said this because I did not want to talk about texting, and calorie counting on menus was a neat idea. It is like a speedometer. If you are going grossly over the speed limit you will know it. Of course knowing you are speeding does not make you slow down. It only gives you the knowledge that you are breaking the laws of common sense, like ordering a large hamburger with fries and a shake every day. But it is still nice to know how many calories you are having when you are having too many.

"Do your friends have diabetes yet?" asked the Earth.

"Of course not. My three friends are in their twenties."

"Wait until they are in their thirties," said the Earth.

A dog walker walked by with an army of dogs surrounding her legs. She carried many plastic bags each containing something warm and heavy flopping up and down on her belt. The dogs' owners were at work sitting at their desks. Their entire day would be spent sitting. At night they would sit. But their dogs would be exercised. That is good.

"Look at how healthy these animals are," I said.

"Those ones don't count," said the Earth. "They have owners rich enough to take over doing what they should be doing. But there is an epidemic of obese dogs. They are getting sick. They can't get up. They eat, and that is all they do."

"But we have organic raw meat for them now," I said.

"You are cutting down forests to make pastures to raise cows to feed dogs that are fat. You are not winning points with me," said the Earth.

"What do you want me to do?" I said.

I was angry. Every single thing we have done for the Earth it twisted around until it sounded bad. I was getting the feeling the Earth thought it was smarter than us. Ha, we have brains. We have inventions. We have cell phones that we can write notes on. What does the Earth have besides some grass and trees and fish that can't even type?

"You figure it out," said the Earth. "I have been through this before. I have survived being hit by an asteroid bigger than a breadbox. And I have survived big-time freeze-ups and big-time meltdowns. I have been through volcanoes blowing up like fireworks factories."

"So, you are tough. Then you can survive us," I said.

"But every time some super-bad thing happened, all my little friends wound up in a museum with their bones on display."

"Is this a super-bad time?" I asked.

A garbage truck passed by with twenty tons of used diapers and other wet things heading for a hole in the ground in Cache Creek that makes a lot of money by taking other people's garbage, which is a growth industry. The trucks are in a previous story.

Another truck was following. And a third after that. The only job the trucks have is moving Vancouver's garbage to a small town up north. The trucks are longer than a tractor trailer and are filled to the top.

"Super-bad time," said the Earth.

"So, what should we do?" I asked. "We have bike lanes now."

The Earth grunted. It was the first human thing it had done during the whole conversation.

"You figure it out," it said again. "You say you have brains, right? You are smarter than the grass, right? You figure it out."

Then the Earth went quiet.

"But what should we do?" I was talking to the tree. A Park Ranger in a hybrid pickup truck stopped.

"What are you doing?" said the ranger after he rolled down his electric-powered window.

"Nothing," I said.

"It looked like you were talking to that tree."

"Are you kidding?" I said. "I was just wondering why the leaves on the tree were dying, and it's only springtime."

"We'll give it some fertilizer and it will be fine," he said. Then he drove off.

I turned and walked away but a second later I heard a grunt. I turned my head back to the tree, but the only thing I saw was a leaf falling. Fertilizer will fix it, I thought. That is the way we fix everything.

The Wool Machine

I t was not beautiful just because it was old. It was beautiful because it was old and still working.

One hundred and thirty years ago a workman put together several large drums, big enough for a ten-year-old to crawl inside, and added some metal teeth to make combs and then attached large leather belts to turn the drums and it did stuff you could not believe.

It carded wool. Put the raw wool in at one end and the teeth in its combs ran over and over it until a smooth, flat blanket of wool came out the other end. Amazing.

"Ten people working all day could not do what this machine does in an hour," said someone in the 1880s.

It was amazing. It was in the time when machines were starting to replace hands and arms.

"It was just born, but we'll call it the old lady," someone said.

And the name stuck. It was the Old Lady, sometimes the Old

Girl, from then on. It had a personality. It was big. In the beginning it was run by power from a creek that pushed pedals that turned a small drum around on which the belts were placed. They turned the big drums on the Old Lady.

Later it was powered by steam.

In 1938 it was brought to Vancouver by the grandfather of Cara Birkeland. He bought a small shop on Main Street for $700 (yes, $700) and in the backroom he put the Old Lady together. There were more pieces than just a few big drums. More than twenty rollers, each more than six feet long, had to be reassembled.

Forget the comparison with IKEA furniture, which you have to put together using instructions with no words and which you sometimes get done. And don't try to compare the Old Lady with assembling an integrated circuit on a motherboard from a schematic drawing that hurts the eyes and the brain. The Old Lady came in pieces with no instructions.

"My grandfather, Olaf, took a long time to get it together," said Cara Birkeland.

She grew up watching her grandfather, and then her father, stand at one end of the machine, feeding the rough wool in and then, a few minutes later, taking the smooth quilt stuffing out at the other.

The floor where her grandfather and later her father stood, and where Cara now stood, was worn through the plywood and onto the support beams below.

I found this story about the old machine fascinating, but what did I really like about it? I liked what I knew about it. I liked the belts that went around and around and kept it going. I liked that because when I was a boy we had no money. I am not complaining or bragging—no one had any money—but when my shoes wore out I went to the shoemaker to get them fixed.

I walked twenty blocks, a normal distance for anyone to walk then, to a big train station where a shoe-fix-it shop was right outside waiting for the passengers. Everyone walked then. That is why everyone got their shoes fixed back then.

I would take off my shoes at the counter and hand them to the man with the rough fingers who stood on the other side of the glass counter that had pictures of shoes and soles and heels with the company name of Cat's Claws (a great name for shoe bottoms) on the other side of the glass.

When my shoes needed fixing the soles were gone and the heels were worn down to the point where there was no more heel.

"Take a seat," the shoemaker would say.

Behind me was a row of chairs. I sat beside men in suits whose feet had only socks. They were reading newspapers. I was not reading. I was watching the machines that were powered by one overhead spinning pipe. The machines the shoemakers were working on had leather belts that went up to the pipe. When a man wanted to start his machine he slipped the belt onto a spool and the machine started moving instantly. Mostly they were sewing machines.

There were about seven men fixing shoes and each had a sewing machine and each had a belt and each slipped them on and off. It was a ballet, even though I had never heard the word.

They ripped the soles and heels off my shoes with pliers, then painted glue on the bottoms and slapped on new heels and soles. Next came some trimming, and then a hand went up and moved the belt onto a spool and started sewing the bottom of my shoes.

Twenty minutes later I was handed my new soles and heels with the old top, good for another two or three months or until my feet got too big for them.

Every time I walked back home I wanted to walk around the world with my new bottoms.

More than half a century later when I saw the belts on the wool machine I could only think of my shoes. There is nothing wrong with that. That is the way we are made.

When Cara sees the belts she thinks of her grandfather and her father and a little girl, herself, working behind it.

You can see how the machine worked by going to the website of Birkeland Wool. You can see the story, but you will probably see something else, too, something no one else knows about. You may see your grandmother making a quilt from combed wool. You never knew how the wool turned out that way, you only knew that your grandmother made the best, most comfortable quilts in the world.

The machine was taken apart in the spring of 2012 because Cara's health was bad and her doctor had told her she could no longer work. It took days and many volunteers to undo what her grandfather had done by himself.

The Old Lady is now resting in Abbotsford waiting to be put together again, to have the belts attached again and to start carding wool again. When it does, I will do a story about it. The art is that something keeps going. But the real story, as with everything, is the story that you see in that art.

The Weaving Hands

Many of the stories in here are too long, and I apologize. I just forget to stop writing, but here's a short one, about a woman who takes a long, long time to do each of the pieces that she creates.

She takes one strand of hand-spun wool and weaves it through a series of tight vertical strings. That would be the technical way of saying she does tapestry, one hand-spun, hand-dyed strand at a time, weaving back and forth with only her fingers guiding and pulling the wool.

Barbara Heller weaves in the same way as medieval tapestry weavers—just hands, eyes and wool. And patience, and design, and … "Darn."

"What?" I ask.

"A hangnail. You get that doing this."

She is wonderful. I am watching a piece of art that will sell for $15,000 being created before my eyes, and the artist is so human.

"What do you do now?" I asked, thinking that this is a major breakdown of the main part of the machinery.

"I file it down. What do you think I do?"

Behind her are faces pressed against the window of her studio, which is on Granville Island. They watch knowing something beautiful is going on and yet it is so simple. Part of the beauty is in the simplicity.

"In the afternoons I have to clean off the smudges of little noses and fingerprints," she said.

Those are from the children who watch. They want to get closer. The adults know the rule: Don't Touch. We lose so much enjoyment when we grow up and follow the rules.

Back to Barbara. She is either one of the country's leading tapestry makers or *the* leading tapestry maker in the country. It depends on whether humility or truth takes the lead.

"It is funny about the twists and turns of life," she said.

When her art career started, tapestry was not her art. She wanted more than anything to do silkscreen printing. This was in the early years of silkscreen, forty years ago. She was happy and creative and successful.

"It was also at a time when ventilation was not high on the list of things to think about," she said.

Paint fumes are not good when they get inside the lungs. She got sick, and then sicker, but she kept working, which is what people do when they are dedicated to what they do.

Finally the diagnosis was double pneumonia, or simply "very sick."

Her doctor said no more silkscreen.

She looked around for something else, and there it was in a pile of yarn.

"Funny about the twists and turns of life," she repeated.

There is more to the story. Like the medieval tapestry artists who put royal and church stories into their work, Barbara puts in images that say we should clean up the rivers and lakes before we kill all the fish, or we should stop wars before we do the same to ourselves. And if you don't like social conscience hung on your wall, then she does weavings of flowers and hillsides and peacefulness.

And there is the reality that her works sell for high prices but that when she figures how long she takes to make them, she is working for minimum wage or less. That is one of those endless ironies that we hear and then we grunt, like we suddenly understand the real meaning of life.

But in short, go watch her. Press your nose against the window. She is on Granville Island, very easy to find. From her fingers you will follow the twists and turns of yarn, and if she suddenly stops and says "Darn," you can tell the others who are watching, "Hangnail. Occupational hazard."

My Druggist,
the American TV Commercial

You know that the airwaves are filled with ads for prescription drugs. The street-level drug dealers are not the only ones who are making money from life-changing chemicals, but on television the drug companies have to, by law, include the side effects.

I have just watched a commercial about a new drug that cures skin blemishes. It came from the US, where blemishes are apparently a growing concern for aging people. They have to worry about something besides not having a pension.

Skin problems were traditionally the nightmare of teenagers who had to face the dread of going on a date with a new pimple on their nose.

"No, mom, no. I can't go out with Simon with this zit. Please put me out of my misery. Please lock me in my room. Please go to the drugstore and get me something."

And mother went to the store and got Susie something that

covered the pimples and something else that would get rid of them in six months, which was about the same time as nature would take.

Then Simon showed up with hungry eyes and a vibrating heart and two cheeks that looked like coarse red sandpaper. Susie and Simon had a wonderful night at the movies, where pimples were the only subject that did not come up.

Susie and Simon are now retired and worried. They have blemishes, once again. Susie does not want to be seen as a senior citizen with zits, and Simon, who does not mind the senior part, is afraid people will think he has returned to some behaviour that supposedly gave him zits when he was fourteen.

In the commercial on American television, Susie is flying to a school reunion. She is in Business Class—we know because she has only one person sitting next to her. This tells us she has made it in every way, except for those life-altering blemishes.

Simon is playing tennis at the country club, so we know he has achieved what he had hoped for, but in the commercial we see the glances of the men he is playing with. They are obviously thinking Simon is not in control of his life. One of them looks at a friend, glances at Simon and then points to his own cheek.

It is beyond amazing what you can do in fifteen seconds.

Then come the voice-over warnings, which are required by law.

"If you take this medicine you may experience forgetfulness, hypertension and anxiety."

The screen now shows Susie arriving at her reunion, the centre of attention, with clear skin. Cut to Simon, with glowing cheeks, defeating his opponents who cannot keep up with his serves.

The voice-over continues: "If you take this medicine you may experience kidney failure and liver damage as well as erectile dysfunction."

But the makers of the message know no one is listening. Simon has just made an impossible play and adoring eyes are all on Susie's clear cheeks.

"If you take this medicine you may develop cancer of the colon ..."

Susie shows great surprise at seeing someone she obviously had not expected to see and who is undoubtedly the most handsome man at the reunion, and as they hug we see she has no wedding ring.

Did she never marry Simon? Is she cheating? No, not in a commercial. She has at last found love.

That is followed by Simon's arms held high over his head with the racquet in one hand ...

"... and possible brain cancer, which can lead to death."

Susie and her new man look into each other's eyes and Simon leaps over the net to unseen applause.

Get me that medicine. I cannot live with these aging blemishes. Plus I may meet Susie. Or at the worst, I will be able to jump over a net like Simon.

Death? I didn't hear that part.

Green Snow Doesn't Taste So Good.
Whoops.

"Sure you can eat it." That was me, grandpa who knows everything, telling Ruby, granddaughter who believes grandpa knows everything, that of course she could eat the green snow.

She had a spray bottle with green water made by her grandmother who knows even more than grandpa. She also knows all about kids and how to keep them excited about everything. I got the spray bottle from a closet that has all sorts of things grandmother makes for kids.

"Will it hurt the plants under the snow?" Ruby asked.

"Of course not," I said. Her grandmother would never hurt anything, least of all plants shivering under icy snow.

"This is just food colouring, the same as goes on cookies and cakes," I told the trusting and believing Ruby.

"Can I eat it?"

"Of course."

She tasted some green snow.

"Yuck, pooey, yucky."

This cannot be, I thought. Grandmother is never wrong. Grandpa is never wrong, except sometimes.

"Try over there," I said, thinking that the fault must be in the snow and I did not want to think about that.

She sprayed and tasted.

"Yuck. It is the same. It tastes terrible," said Ruby.

Grandmother came outside and I told her the green snow did not taste good.

"You didn't tell her she could eat it?" she said.

Well, no. Well, yes. "But it's just food colouring, right?"

"*No!* It is food colouring with dish soap. Then it washes out of their clothes."

"Whoops. Sorry, Ruby. But the good news is now you can tell your little sister not to eat the green snow. She will think you know everything."

Thankfully, There Are Still Kings and Queens

"Can we play checkers?"

"Checkers?"

She nodded.

"You mean with actual pieces on a board, checkers?"

She nodded again.

Music, symphony, art, everything! Rejoice! An eight-year-old girl, my granddaughter, asked if we could play an actual game—not in virtual space.

"Yes, of course we can play, yes, right away. Do you know how to play?" I asked, because I had never played with her and never seen her play with anyone else.

"I learned it on the computer," she said.

This is Ruby coming of age in an age when boards will be no more.

"You once said that you had a checkers game," she added.

"Yes, I do, somewhere."

Now I am desperate because I want so much to play checkers with her, to slide the little plastic discs around and look for a double jump and say, "Darn, I did not see that" when someone else double jumps me.

Somewhere there is a board. Not in the back of the closet. No, but there are some shoes in there that I did not remember. And there are some dust balls that must have sneaked in just yesterday because I would never have allowed them to build up like that.

And the old checkers box is not under the bed. There are other things under there that I don't remember putting there but I know the checkers is not there because the game is in a box with the word Checkers and a picture of a happy family standing around a board while a brother and sister play and the family looks like this is the most exciting thing in the world. There *was* hype before there were computers.

But downstairs, in the backroom of downstairs, on top of the old home-made bookcase that's behind the IKEA sofa, which was put there because no one could sit on it without sliding off, was the happy family.

It was under some *National Geographic* magazines that were under the remains of an old paper and balsa wood airplane that was made by her great-grandfather, whom she never met.

"What's that?" Ruby asked.

"An old airplane that your mommy's grandfather made and was going to fix."

"Can I fly it?"

"Just as soon as I fix it."

"When is that?"

"When I get a chance."

"Let's play checkers," she said. She is very smart. She understands grandfathers.

There's no problem setting up the game. She knows how the pieces go and how they move and jump.

"Is this better than a computer?" I ask.

"Slower," she answers as she double jumps me.

"Can we play that other game, the one with the funny pieces, on this board?"

Chess? Do you, at eight, want to learn chess? I think.

Of course.

I have had a chess set since I was fifteen, same set, same board, same instructions inside the box.

"Ugh, what's this?" asked Ruby as she opened the box and looked at the brown, crinkly, decaying paper that was once the instructions.

"That tells you how to play," I said.

"But I thought you knew."

Right. And now I am in a quandary. Do I throw out those instructions just because they are falling apart? They are more than a half a century old. They could be worth something, someday, maybe. I can't throw them out. Maybe I can fix them with some tape.

I lift the paper out carefully and roll out the chess pieces that will soon go into battle.

"Is that a clown?"

"No, it's a bishop."

"Is that his mouth?"

"No, it's a hat."

Chess, which is the world's oldest thinking game and still the world's most popular, has crazy rules and invites crazy people to play it.

"Is that a horse?"

"No, it's a knight."

"Why does it look like a horse?"

"Because knights rode horses."

"So did cowboys."

When it became a world craze a few decades ago, with the best of America and Russia competing, there were complaints by some players of telepathic signals being sent by other players. One player had all the fillings in his teeth drilled out because he thought someone was sending radio signals to him to mess up his game. The signals were coming through the fillings.

I worked with one man at the *New York Daily News* who was one of their battery of fast-typing hard crime writers. He could turn out three pages of blood and murder in about fifteen minutes, and he was highly paid for this skill, but he lived not for crime or writing or newspapers, but for chess.

He brought his cardboard playing field and his set of plastic chess pieces with him every night and played with anyone he could find who wanted to go up against him. That was between killings and deadly crashes. If no one was available to play, he would make a move, turn the board around and play against himself.

All fairly normal, so far. But he would not change his shirt. The collar was worn so thin his tie was coming through the fold at the top of the collar. He must have washed it, because he didn't smell, but it was the same shirt for the two years I knew him.

He lived in a one-room four-storey walk-up because it was near the Marshall Chess Club in Manhattan. That is one of the oldest and most famous chess clubs in America. Bobby Fischer, who had the fillings taken out of his teeth, was a member.

My friend played there every day. And he played with his own chess set. He would not play with anything else, although it was the cheapest of cheap plastic. He had taken it to the printing floor of the newspaper, where he talked someone into filling the inside of each of the pieces with the melted zinc that was used to make the type for the papers.

"It helps me," was all he said.

One time he talked to me about something other than chess and murder.

"I've found that if you buy chicken backs and necks you can get them for close to nothing and then boil them and have soup for a week."

He was lean. He did not want to spend money because, you never know. "Like with chess," he said, "life always has something you did not plan for."

One shirt, zinc in his king, and chicken necks. Other sports do not have players like that.

Despite all that, I was thrilled when Ruby said she wanted to learn.

We began with the pawn moves forward, but takes another piece to the diagonal, and the pawn can move forward two spaces on the first move, but not on the second.

That she got without a why. That was saved for castle. "Why is it at the end? Don't the king and queen live in the castle?"

Yes, but it goes at the end.

If the king is so important why can he only move one space?

If the queen can move anywhere why is she not in charge?

Why does a bishop look like a clown?

And real horses cannot jump to the side.

Those are all good questions. I am sure my friend back at the newspaper could answer them, or he would change the subject to chicken necks.

So we started, and the horses tripped and the clown got lost and the queen strayed and we had the best game I ever had.

"Can we play checkers again?" Ruby asked.

That was just when her little sister Zoe came by and reached up to the table and grabbed a horse, which is a knight, and rode away with it.

Ruby got a double jump. I lost. On the other hand, someday she will teach someone about checkers, or maybe even chess. And I know that by then she will understand that the queen really is in charge.

A Free Course on Writing

Let me tell you about writing. Let me tell you how one little thing can change your life. They go together like everything goes together.

Many of you want to be writers. There is nothing to it. You get a notebook and a Bic pen and write until you have a callus on one of your fingers that is thicker than leather.

I had that, and I was proud of my callus. It was better than my writing. I was just holding a pen and making words and writing about the meaning of life, mine, and how much I wanted to be a writer and wondering if anyone would ever read this and I pretended I was a great writer, except by then I was dead and I couldn't write any more.

I wanted to be a writer because I thought it was mysterious. It was the witch's kettle brewing with something. You didn't know what would come out of it, but it was magical. I wanted to be a writer because I wanted to work for a newspaper and the reporters had to stand in the rain. The writers worked indoors.

I wanted to be a writer because I could not write (I have told you before that I didn't read a book until I was fourteen) and my first attempt at being a writer was a failure. They tried me on the rewrite desk and I didn't know where to begin the stories or end them or what to put in the middle. I could not compose a simple sentence, and when you work for a tabloid they use only simple sentences. So I became a reporter and stood in the rain and gathered the information about the murders and car crashes and stood in a phone booth and called the city room and spoke to a writer who was warm and dry and wrote the story.

Then, on the GI Bill (you've heard of that—it was the US government's way of paying back its soldiers and sailors by giving them money to go to college), I went to college and signed up for a course in writing.

Our first assignment was to write something. I had just gotten out of uniform and was walking through the streets of Brooklyn thinking of what to do for my homework. It was raining. I had only a raincoat and it was a New York winter, which is much the same as a Toronto or Ottawa winter. It was cold. I was cold. What can I write about?

I saw, by the curb of a street, a boy huddled over a dead dog. The dog was like a dam for the water that was flowing along the gutter. Behind it was piled-up cigarette packages and gum wrappers. The boy was petting the dog's head.

"Hello, what you doing?" I asked.

He looked up. Rain was falling on his face. He did not care. He wore only a thin coat and it was soaked.

"He was my dog," he said.

He told me he had found the dog wandering the streets a few days before and had given him a cookie he had in his pocket. Then he went into a corner grocery and bought a tiny container of milk and some more cookies. The dog was waiting for him outside and the boy ripped open the top of the milk container and the dog took less than a minute to lap it up. The boy said he had to hold the container so the dog wouldn't knock it over. Then he gave him the cookies.

He went home to his apartment. It was in a project. Some people in Vancouver tell me they grew up in the projects and have good memories of the friends they made there. They have no idea about projects.

He went home to a thirty-storey building with bars on every window on the first three floors. Even burglars didn't get to be taller than that. But something else was in every hallway up to the thirtieth floor—urine. Every door to every apartment looked the same as the ones they used in prisons for solitary confinement. There were no trees or grass in front of the building.

The boy came back with a piece of rope and the dog was waiting for him.

He tied the rope around the dog's neck and they ran down the street. They ran around the corner. They ran and played and he used the last of his money to buy some more milk and cookies.

Then he brought the dog home. That was forbidden. There were no animals allowed in the projects. But he did it anyway. And the dog slept on his bed.

His mother did not know because his mother did not tuck him in at night. She was doing other things. That was the way it was in the projects.

The next day they played, and the next. The boy didn't go to school. Many of the kids in projects didn't go to school. I didn't go to school when I was his age. That is a problem. Some kids don't go to school because they cannot figure out what is going on in school. You solve that problem and you have solved many problems.

Then, on the third day in the late afternoon in the rain when it was getting dark, the boy and his dog were running along the sidewalk when the rope slipped from the boy's hand. The dog kept going and ran out into the street, looking back to see if the boy was following him and the headlights of a car saw the dog, and the boy saw the headlights and his dog... long pause ... come together.

Bam. Thunt. Choose a word. It doesn't matter what it sounds like. It was a thud, or whatever you want to say, and the dog went flying like a ball off a bat or a dog off a bumper and landed by the curb.

Later that night the boy went home. Or at least I imagined he did. I was sure he would have gotten tired or cold.

It was the next morning that I saw him petting the dog's head in the rain.

"Hello, what are you doing?"

He told me what had happened. Then he went back to petting its head.

I went on to work. I was a young reporter at the *New York Daily News*, the largest circulation newspaper in America. I was on the bottom rung. I could not write. This was in the old days when reporters were not expected to write. They reported. They stayed outside. The writers inside the newsroom wrote. And yes, I did start in the mail room and work my way up, but there was no expectation that I would ever move from seeing things happen to recording the things for others to see.

My homework was due the next day. The assignment was to write a story on some current event. I wrote about the boy and his dog. That was current. I wrote it on a typewriter (Grandpa, what's a typewriter?) that had large keys. The typewriters used by the writers of the old-time newspapers had letters five times bigger than the type you are reading. The publishers understood that the editors, who were the magician of the stories, were either hungover or going blind. Both were traditional.

I still did not know how to write, so I simply typed out what the boy told me.

Two classes later the teacher held up the papers that had been handed in. He said he did not usually single anyone out, but this was different.

I was not hoping for anything except the class to end. I smelled of cigarettes and coffee. I had been out on the street reporting all night. I just wanted to go home and get into bed.

He started to read. "A dog lay in a puddle next to the curb. A young boy was petting his head."

Holy unbelievable. I stayed awake. He read the whole paper. No one in the class moved. If you want a crowning moment in life you got it, right there. Or at least I had it. I slid down in my seat. I did not want anyone to know it was me. I don't know why, but I did not.

"But it is not written on a conventional typewriter. For that he will lose five points. And for poor spelling he will lose five more points. And for punctuation five more. And for sloppy work (coffee stains on the paper) five more."

"What?" I had no idea what he was talking about, but never be surprised by rule 1-B, which you did not know about but that contradicts rule 1-A, which makes coffee stains important.

No one in the class knew it was me. No one would have cared. Like the other part-time commuting students I came and went unnoticed.

Despite all the deductions I got an A, with the comment that it was a good first draft.

Are you kidding, I thought. In my world the first draft is the only draft. But I did not say that. I took the paper and wanted to keep it but I lost it—the only school paper I got in my entire life that I liked and I never saw it again.

But shortly afterwards, during one of the nasty racial riots of the early 1970s, I was near a massive crowd fighting with police on the street. Instead of reporting about the fighting, the big story, I thought of the boy and the dog.

I looked around, no dog, just police. I looked to the end of the street, more police. I looked at the end of the street in the other direction, rioters.

I looked up, and there was a woman leaning out of her fourth-floor window watching the ugly, scary battle.

I went to the apartment and knocked. She talked to me through the door. I told her who and what I was and why I wanted to talk to her—just to see how she was and what she thought of it all.

She opened three locks, but did not take off the security chain. When the door opened about the width of my thumb I could see her face on the other side of the chain. I thanked her. I showed her some identification. I told her I only wanted to know how the street had changed, and how long she had lived there, and what she thought about anything or everything.

She said she could not let me in. I said this was fine. I wrote the story and offered it to the editors. I wrote it just as she said it, very simply, one person, one world that has changed and one fear.

The next day the story in the newspaper about the interview through the crack in the door got more comments than the main, big-time stories on the riot.

The following day the rioting was still going on and I sat on the ground under a police wooden barricade and talked to one police-man. I had to stay out of his line of sight because he was watching for things being thrown at him. One cop, one job, many things being thrown. The story became a major feature in the Sunday paper. And I wrote it. I wrote just what he said while he kept his eyes on others.

And then I talked to one of the rioters, a very angry fellow much younger than me and I was not yet thirty. At the office they said they were waiting for the story. One person, one endless stream of anger and frustrations and unfair treatment. It was not hard to write.

Now jump ahead ten, twenty, thirty years. You watch the stories on the television. What are they about? Right, mostly one person do-ing one thing. The big difference now of course is they are usually in a garden or flying a kite or playing with a grandchild. That is because nice stories are better for your health.

But as far as writing them? Simple. Just find the story, and the story will write itself. And how do you find the story? Talk to someone. Try it.

Now, How to Really Do the Job

"Can you tell me what you are doing?"

What I saw were three young kids, but they were doing something. One was a reporter with a microphone asking questions. One was a young lady with a camera standing behind him. The other was standing there looking like she was ready to help.

The person being asked the questions walked away.

"It is hard to talk to the young ones," said Kyle.

Kyle was ten. The person being asked was maybe seven.

"So what do you do then?" asked older reporter, also with a microphone and with someone behind him with a camera.

"Go on and find someone else," said Kyle.

That is wonderful. That is super. Kyle, you have just passed the graduate level of Journalism. There is not too much to this job or to life except persistence and an occasional smile.

Kyle was at the Pacific National Exhibition fair. He had a foam rubber toy microphone that, like many real microphones that cost a lot and have wires and batteries and transmitters, was useless if you cannot find someone willing to talk.

"What are you doing?" asked older reporter with microphone, happy that the younger reporter was willing to talk.

"We are getting stories," said younger reporter.

"And what will you do with them?" asked older guy, who was very happy now because not only was our subject talking but he was saying something.

And it did not matter what the answer was because the younger fellow had already said enough to get a conversation going.

You see, in the older fellow's endless days of standing in the rain and sunshine and snow and sleet and sometimes indoors, he had found most people talk but few actually say something interesting. Most talk about themselves and their aches and dislikes. When you meet someone who says he or she is doing something or thinking something or preparing something outside of themselves, you have a winner. People who talk about things other than themselves are interesting, so you listen.

"We will put them on YouTube," said the young lady with the camera, who was about twelve.

"And then what will you have?" asked old guy who started in newspapers and then went to television and has always worked for some giant organization.

"We will have our own television show," said Kyle.

How is this possible? Two kids, brother and sister, Kyle and Jessica, with friend Claire, who was a producer even though neither she nor I knew what a producer did, with a sponge mike and a hand-sized video camera, had broken into a world formally controlled by Networks and Media Empires.

It was true. Many people put things on YouTube, but when you decide what you are doing is a television station or news show or whatever you want to call it, then that is what it is. All at once there was nothing separating what they were doing from what I was doing, except I would get paid for it.

Nonetheless, they would get paid in thrills and prestige and probably an early resumé that would get them hired somewhere they would be paid. Or they would figure out how to get an income just from their stories. I don't know how, but I am sure they will figure it out.

So I watched them. They went on video recording other kids playing and eating and painting an old car that was at the fair with the purpose of being painted.

That was so amazing, because over the past lifetime that I have been doing this I have been asked by many journalism students and practicum students how they can get started in the business. Have you written any stories, I ask? Have you sent any story ideas to magazines? Have you found any stories that could appear on television or radio and gathered them on tape or in words and presented them to an editor?

Usually, no. They, like many, wait for the job and then plan to do it. And yet here were some kids doing it without having the job.

That applies to everything. How many people do you know who want to be a mechanic and hope to get a job in a car company and then are told they have to go to school to learn to be a mechanic before they are hired? So they borrow the money and apply at a school and get put on a waiting list and they say they can't get anywhere because nothing is open for them.

Take away the word mechanic and put in any other field, anything, and how many people do you know fit in that rut?

Then look at the people who were stripping apart lawn mower motors when they were kids, or writing songs, or building dollhouses and then tree houses and then shacks and then repairing doors and windows in their parents' homes.

"I guess you are going to be a carpenter when you get older?" would say the parent.

"I *am* a carpenter," would say the growing child. "I want to build skyscrapers when I get older."

That is like Kyle and Jessica and Claire.

I meant this story to be funny, but it isn't. It is the reality you can learn by watching just about anyone doing anything. The neat thing is when someone is doing something, at any age, and they are not complaining or wishing or moping or talking about what they want to do—they are doing it.

Then I saw Kyle interviewing a biker. He didn't have a motorcycle, but he had a black leather vest over his bare arms and chest and a backward baseball cap with Harley-Davidson written across the front, which was in the back.

He also had tattoos over his arms, each of which was larger than Kyle. He had a girlfriend by his side who also had a black vest and tattoos on her arms.

I am thinking, How the heck did you get the courage to talk to them? Kyle didn't do it because we were watching—he was now way over there and we were left behind way over here. He was off exploring extreme distant horizons in journalism. He was already building his skyscraper.

We got closer and listened.

"How many tattoos do you have?" he asked and pointed his foam rubber mike up at the man with the vest, with a working microphone on the camera.

"Too many to count, but actually more than forty," said the giant with the tattoos.

"Why do you have them?"

The man with the tattoos looked at his girlfriend and smiled. "I really don't know. I started too young and just kept going."

This was groundbreaking. Kyle, who was more than pretending

to do something, was getting into the mind of someone else. He was getting honesty. This would be a hit on YouTube or anywhere.

"Do you wish you didn't have them?" Kyle asked.

"Sometimes," said the man, who had them everywhere.

"Thank you for talking with us, Rick," Kyle said.

I was stunned. Truly. Kyle had gotten his name at the beginning of the interview, making it a personal conversation rather than an interrogation. That is super-advanced journalism school teaching.

Then I asked the man with the tattoos what he thought of Kyle's interviewing skills.

"Very good," he said, of course because we were now asking on camera. Then he said, "but most of all I appreciate that he remembered my name."

Very often reporters and many others will forget who they are talking to. A new name passes by like the wind—it hits you and then it's gone—but Kyle remembered it and thanked Rick by name, which is one of the most thoughtful things anyone can do for anyone else. Hearing your name can make you feel like the other person really cares.

Kyle did that, and Rick was impressed. The reporter with the sponge microphone did not take him for granted.

About at that point I thought Kyle could be teaching journalism. He had determination and consideration. To do anything, you don't really need anything else, except the occasional smile. That black make-believe thing in his hand could have been looked at as a toy or as a tool. He could have pretended it was a microphone or said it *was* a microphone, and whatever you say and believe becomes so.

The Simple Lesson,
and Really It Is So Simple for Two

The PNE was on. This is last year and I am at the Pacific National Exhibition because I want to be there. As I have said so many times, this is a country fair, and since I didn't grow up with country fairs, at the other end of my life I want to be at a country fair.

But what cameraman do I get? Anyone who is not doing sixty-five other assignments. The PNE can wait. The PNE is always there. It's the PNE so we don't have to rush. Those are the words of those who assign cameras.

Wait, here is a brilliant solution. We have two new videographers trying out for jobs. Send them to McCardell.

And so, "Who are you?" I ask the two new videographers.

"We are trying to get jobs," they said, together.

"Good," I said, "What are your qualifications?"

And then they listed off a long list of schools and classes and achievements and other things that you put on a resumé when you are young. The younger you are, the longer the resumé.

"Good," I said. "Take the camera and go out and shoot a story."

"About what?" they said.

"Anything you find."

"Can you give us a lead? Is there a press release?"

"Sorry," I said, "there are no press releases in life and none today. You are on your own. Go forth and find something."

They left with their cameras and I drank water and stayed in the shade. It was a good day.

And then they came back.

"We got it, we hope," one said. "Now it's up to you to see what we got," said the other.

They had pictures of kids riding rides and interviews with kids who said they almost threw up, and pictures of bridesmaids on a woman's last day before joining hands in holy matrimony. And they had talks with the woman who is about to change her life who said she hoped she would not throw up on her wedding dress. That was good. One of them lost his sunglasses and went on a hunt for them, asking people where he should look and they told him to look in the toilet (not there) and in the lost and found, where they found another story.

In the end what they got was very good.

"What did you learn?" I asked. I didn't think they would have learned anything, because they have been to school and studied the finer points of journalism and so must know everything.

"I don't know why I did not know this before, but I should talk to a lot more people in my life," said the one who lost his glasses. "That was so much fun."

And that is all there is to it, or really to anything.

They both used the story on their resumés.

Writing the Story

"**N**o, that is not good enough."

That is an editor speaking while a television story is being written.

"But it is all I have to say. He is carrying a rose and going to give it to someone. So I say 'He has a rose for someone.'"

That is me speaking. Me, who has written 10,000 stories for television and forty pounds of newspaper clippings and eight books (counting this one). Don't ever think writing is easy.

"No, no, no," says the editor, who has never written anything but has corrected and improved 100,000 stories for television. That is what a good editor does. He or she takes something that is okay and makes it Wow!

He slips some licorice into his mouth. He likes licorice. Someone else comes into his room.

"Is that the salty licorice?"

"No, it's plain."

"Can I have some?"

"Take it. Take all you want."

"I don't want a lot, just a taste," says his visitor, who is another editor. "What's the story about?"

"Some guy with a rose. The story's all done. We just need some good writing."

"Can I have some more licorice?"

"I told you, take all you want," said the editor who is working with me.

"If it was a black rose you could say it was a rose unlike any other rose," said the visiting editor, whose tongue was turning black.

"If it was a black rose he would not be giving it to anyone," said the editor who is working with me.

"Well maybe he would if it was a murder plot," said the visiting editor.

Writing is not just words. Writing is experience and I am listening because you never know when you will hear something that someone has pulled up from his past, something you would never have otherwise thought of.

Meanwhile, I am still trying to think of something to say about the rose. We have ten minutes left before it goes on the air and we're still working on the first sentence.

"I once saw a movie about a black rose," said the visiting editor. "There was a lot of killing in that."

"Why don't you get out of here so we can work," said Karl, the working editor, to Ron, the visiting editor.

But Ron wouldn't leave. "If it was black you could say 'a rose that looks like mud can still smell sweet.'"

"Get out of here," said Karl, who was trying to save my career.

"Can I have some more licorice?"

Karl tossed the bag of licorice at him "Go," he said.

Real writing is like that. You have to stop and listen to your kids in the middle of a sentence, and then answer the phone and get coffee when you can't think of the next word. Writing is like living. Things happen. That's what gives it life.

And now we have seven minutes left.

"I don't want to overplay it," I said. "It's just a rose."

"But what colour is it?" he asks me, expecting me to see the obvious because it is right in front of my eyes on the high definition video screen in his edit room.

How do I know what colour it is? I'm colour blind. Honest to the United States Air Force who tested me when I was in basic training. They handed me cards with dots of colours on them and asked me to read the numbers on them.

One, two, I started reading. Three, four. At least I thought I could see three and four.

Then the next card. No number. I thought this was a trick question. They were testing me for my honesty and loyalty if I was captured by the enemy and was forced to confess to acts I did not commit. I was supposed to give only my name, rank and serial number. I should not confess to things I did not do, like flying spy planes.

I saw the card and there was no number. I would answer this honestly. There's no number, sir. No number on that card. And the next one. No number. And the next. Just another card with dots.

I was facing the interrogation of the Russians (because at that time it was the Russians who were the enemy) and I would not be tricked into any answers that I had to invent.

"No number, sir."

The US Air Force sergeant who was giving me the cards put a check on a form on a clipboard and said, "You're colour blind, airman. You will never fly."

"But I joined the Air Force to go into the wild blue yonder," I said.

"What colour is a cloud?" he asked.

"Blue," I said.

"You will be assigned to the pest control squadron, killing mosquitoes," he said.

So after a tour of duty spent spreading DDT (which I knew was white because everyone would say to me after a few hours of blowing the stuff out the back of a truck, "You are all white"), I went back to reporting. Luckily for me that was in a newspaper where everything was black and white.

"It is pink. The rose is pink, you idiot," said the editor. "That's what makes it special. A pink rose for a lady friend."

"I thought roses were red," I said.

"Well this one isn't and that's what makes it special. Did you ask him why he got a pink rose?"

No. I had not asked him. I don't ask anyone about colours. My wife always asks me which colour dress is better and I ask her which one does she like the most and then I say that one is the best colour. So, no, I did not ask him why it was pink.

But he did say that the woman he was giving it to had made everything in her apartment pink.

"Well, that's what you write about. As a master of the obvious, you fail," he said.

I have written about fires, floods and famine. I have reported on crime and love. I have described worms and slugs. But flowers, rainbows and fashion are not on my resumé tape. If I have to write about any of those it is only ever with consultation.

Five minutes to go and I say, "A pink rose for a woman who may blush when she sees soft petals glowing with her favourite colour."

"That's okay," says the editor, which means it is passable, and it gets recorded.

Then we moved on to the second sentence.

Another One of Those Words

It was written on a scrap of cardboard and nailed to a telephone pole.

It was brilliant. If I was writing copy for advertising I would have gotten a bonus for coming up with it. But I could not say it, not professionally. I don't even like it non-professionally.

"You *can* say it," said Gary Woulff. "Go on, try."

He was selling it. He was advertising it. He was making a living off it. He was happy with it.

"I can't," I said.

But I could spell it.

C-R-A-P.

Gary had put up a sign on a telephone pole saying "Garage Sale, Lots of crap for sale."

And the people were lining up to buy.

"Why are you here?" I asked. "It's just a garage sale, like hundreds of others."

"Because there's lots of good crap here," the folks in the line who wanted to buy said.

You cannot beat that for an advertising slogan. It is better than Drink Coca Cola, which is supposed to be the world's best advertisement ever. I read that in some advertising magazine. It said the slogan told you what to do and what to do it with. Simple. And it worked.

But Buy Crap?

"That is neat," said someone else who was buying.

Gary has had many garage sales. He even rented a garage to have them in, he has so much **** to sell. And he's done very well since he started his new ad campaign. He has even had several of his signs stolen, which means they are in demand.

"That's what this stuff is. Some of it is good crap, and some is just crap, but I can't call it anything else," he said.

"But I can't do a story on television about it because I can't say that," I said.

"Try," he said. "It won't hurt."

"I can't."

"Try."

I have scruples. They are not profound, but they are my scruples. I do not want to add bad words to the world.

"Everyone uses it," said Gary.

"Not on television," I said.

Then I had an idea.

"Gary sells C-R-A-P," I said, spelling it.

"I don't like it either," said his wife.

I never said it. His wife never did. But after it was on television he was sold out of that stuff.

I may not like it and I may pretend to have scruples but if you want a lesson in words, there it is. Be inventive. And if you don't like the invention, invent something you do like.

Your Pet Fish

My favourite goldfish was in a soup bowl. I have told you about this before but how could I not mention it again having been in a pet shop today where the fish tank cost $4,000. And that is without the fish.

There is a new kind of interior underwater decorating because there is *always* a new kind of whatever it is that you like. How else can anyone get you to buy more of whatever it is that you like unless they come up with something *new*?

This new kind of fish tank has plants and rocks and gravel, like your old tank, but your old tank did not have them arranged with the new theory of plants and rocks and gravel.

"To do this is to do art," said Joseph Uy, who is the president and owner of Miyabi Aqua Design Ltd., a company that does just this.

And we all know that art is priceless. Or about $4,000 per tank.

In addition to his rocks and gravel and plants, there is a carpet of grass over the gravel, flower beds next to the rocks, and taller plants in the back and the sides. "But not just on the sides," said Joe.

"It is a balance of dividing into thirds, like your fingers are divided into thirds, and your face with your eyes, your nose and your mouth is divided into thirds, and so the tank will be divided into thirds," he said. "And one third must be here, not there," he said pointing to one third of the tank. It is not easy to learn art.

But you see immediately that your rocks and plants and gravel were just there, where you put them. You liked it and it was beautiful and the kids spent hours watching the fish swim around the rocks and plants, but you never knew if you had the wrong third, or worse, no third at all.

"It is Miyabi," a word that Joe said is hard to translate and harder to explain but means ultimate beauty, but it's really much more than that, which is why it is hard to explain.

It is sort of like the beauty of bonsai trees, which are hard to explain once you get past the "it's real small" explanation.

This is a bonsai garden under water. And to do the gardening there are special scissors and pinchers. One hundred and fifty dollars for the scissors, made of the same steel as samurai swords, which is good when clipping plants under water. "Of course if money is an issue there are cheaper ones," said Joe. But his face said you would not really want to buy those. Someone might find out.

One other thing with the new aquarium: "The fish no longer matter," said Joe. "They should be small, like birds flying over the fields, but fish are not the object of this setting."

See, there is always something new.

That is just like the goldfish that one kid named Buster had when we were all kids. His mother had won it at Bingo and he wanted to show us. None of us had ever seen a real live goldfish before.

It was in a soup bowl on his kitchen table. It wasn't doing anything except moving its fins and mouth.

"That's beautiful," said Dorothy, who thought everything was beautiful.

"I wonder what it eats?" someone else said.

And that was when someone got some lettuce and tore off tiny pieces and dropped them into the bowl. The poor fish did not move. We thought maybe it couldn't see them because they were floating on the top so we put in some more lettuce.

It was a little hard to see the fish, but someone else said it probably eats bread. So we got a slice of Wonder Bread, which Builds Strong Bodies 8 Ways, the package said. "That would be good for fish," said the fellow who got the bread.

We picked out squishy crumbs and rolled them between our fingers and dropped them in the bowl. They floated, too, so we started poking them to make them sink. Then we put in more bread.

The bowl was filling up with bread and lettuce when someone said, "Maybe it needs air."

So we brought it outside. More kids came because it is not every day that you get a chance to see a real live goldfish. Kids started pushing each other to get close enough to take a look and Buster said, "Be careful," and more kids came.

Then a bunch of boys from another street happened to be passing by and they squeezed in and there was more pushing and, "Oh, no."

The bowl tipped and Buster was standing right over a sewer. Of course he should not have been standing there. Of course he should have looked first and planned on avoiding that accident. Of course. But most of us are not born very smart and we make mistakes.

"My mother's going to kill me," Buster cried. He really did. You cannot lose your mother's new goldfish when you are nine years old and not cry.

We told him it would be all right. We would catch the fish and she would never know. Dorothy said she knew how. She had been fishing once with her grandfather, who was from Yugoslavia.

She ran home and came back with string and some safety pins. We sat around that sewer through half of that day and half the next year, fishing on a city street and getting stories that some of us still tell. We never did catch the missing fish and Buster's mother was forgiving, but that sewer and that one fish was like Miyabi, which is hard to translate and harder to explain. The memory, at least, is ultimate beauty, but really much more than that. And it did not cost a penny.

The Grand Slam

|t was a grand slam home run.

Do you know there are about half of you who do not know what a grand slam is? For the half who grew up with the grand slam, it's the best thing that can happen in baseball.

The other half grew up on another planet. That is hard to believe, but I keep meeting them and they have no idea. They are otherwise normal, nice people. They love hockey. That is good. They watch football and would not miss the Super Bowl. They send their kids to play soccer.

They even like basketball, because, well, because it is trendy. Movie stars go to basketball games. They go because they either like it or like being seen, and they are indoors and they get front row seats, which in basketball means they are on television every six shots.

But baseball is fading, even in America, where it is the national pastime. If you watch a game on TV during the regular season you can see the stands are empty. You have to look quickly because the camera operators are told not to shoot wide shots that show no one is there.

And so many of you honestly do not know what a grand slam is.

Baseball lesson: Your team is losing. You are three runs behind. It is near the end of the game. Your side gets a little bobbling single and you have one player on first base. But you have two outs and one guy on first is not going to help.

The next fellow up hits a grounder between first and second and it escapes all gloves and now you have someone on first and someone on second.

That's when the hand with the popcorn moves out of the bag but the eyes stay on the field.

It could be, just could be that your team has a chance.

Bang. A hit to the left field and the fielder goes back, back, back and the ball hits the wall and bounces onto the ground and the runners are running, then stopping. A man on first, one on second and third on third.

And then the scrawny player comes up to bat. He could be a pinch-hitter, a substitute, but in baseball sometimes you go by your feeling.

The scrawny player swings and ...

It was like that at the Little Mountain Little League field.

"Stop," I said to Chester Ptasinski, the cameraman. "Did you see that?"

"Of course I saw it. Do you think you are the only one who sees things? What did you see?"

"The people by the fence."

"I saw them before you did."

There is nothing like competitive seeing.

"Well, are you going to stop?"

"Where?"

"Here."

"In the middle of the street?"

Getting out of the van was like being caught in the baseline with two players throwing the ball back and forth trying to tag you out and you trying to get past one of them, either of them, it doesn't matter, without getting hit on the arm by the ball. Stop!

"No."

All of life is a sport and everything is a game, if you want it to be.

"Just stop. Let me out."

Over there, across the street, was a sight that could make baseball hearts giddy. Six guys and one woman were standing next to a fence watching a game. They were way past first base, going out to right field. The stands with the wooden benches were way over there, close up to the action. That's where the moms and dads and sisters and brothers were sitting.

But these fans were standing. That alone was good enough.

"Excuse me," etc. "Why are you standing?"

They looked at me. "Because there's no seats out here."

"But really. Why here?"

You could hear the pleading in my voice, and then I saw the potential grand slam. Oh, lord, please let it happen.

In among those by the fence was a cop. A real, uniformed Vancouver City policeman, gun and badge, no hat, earplug in his ear, watching the game. Right there, the best story of the year. Well, at least for the day.

It has been years, decades actually, since I have seen policemen acting like people. They are so controlled, so watched, so organized, so restricted that the last old cop on the beat is eighty years old and blind. He was in my last book, Whistling Bernie Smith. Read about him if you get a chance. He is wonderful.

But over the past few decades the average police officer has stopped talking to reporters. Forbidden, actually. Everything comes out of the official spokespeople.

The Mounties are beyond belief. We can only interview senior

Mounties and then only if they have a hat on their heads. If we take pictures of Mounties doing police work without their hats they will ask us not to use them. And they will be adamant about it. We can never talk to anyone who is not able to give an official press release.

And most of all, none of them would stand by a Little League field watching a game, for fear that someone might see them. Anyway, they are so undermanned and overworked they have no time to watch baseball.

The city police are pretty much the same, except they don't worry about their hats if they are in the process of arresting someone or putting down a riot. But as for talking to us, no, never, not on your life, at least not in front of a camera. "You can get the information from the spokesperson, later."

That is just the trend of the world. In the past year the Park Board has forbidden its employees from talking to the media. Gardeners are not allowed to talk to me about dandelions. Yes, that is true. Lifeguards are not allowed to talk about the weather. We must first get approval from the public relations department of the Park Board and inform them what questions we will ask.

It is beyond anything my head can understand. Almost no one is allowed to speak because they might say something. Of course you always want the official version, but the unofficial one is also unfiltered and hasn't been moulded to fit with policy.

The same with the School Board. We cannot ask workers dismantling old school desks about the initials written on the plastic that is supposed to look like wood. "No," we were told. "You must get permission from our public relations department before you ask about the heart drawn on a desk."

When we called the officials they did not call us back. They were up to our tricks.

The awful part of this is the Park Board and the School Board are not forbidding *us* access. They are forbidding *you*. The only insight you can get from them now is their official press releases, which never contain an oddball question.

This started in the courts and hospitals and federal government and moved down to the local levels. When I did a story about brave garbage men wearing pink vests on Pink Shirt Day there were memos flying around the sanitation department asking how this could happen without the approval of officials.

You can agree or not that this is good. You can say that reporters nose around where they are not wanted. That is what reporters should do. You can disagree with me. My only point is, this is reality.

The other point is there was a city cop watching baseball, like a real human being.

"Do you mind if we take a picture of you all?" I asked.

The group laughed, groaned, snickered like a group would do. "Sure," one of them said. Then the cop said, "I'll just slide away."

The rest laughed, because they knew it would be out of character for a policeman to be photographed doing something other than doing things by the book.

"It would be very good if you stood there," I said.

He shook his head.

"It would be very good public relations for people to see you on your lunch break watching kids play baseball."

There must have been something magical about the word baseball. He walked back to the fence and joined the others. The good news is that, with all the complaining I have just done about the world closing up, he said we could take his picture, without prior approval. A minute later he said, on camera, that he had played baseball as a kid and it was in his blood. And, like the others, he had no children on the field. They were all just fans who stood by a fence for a few innings and watched something they love.

The skinny kid had come to the plate with the bases loaded and swung his bat at the exact moment when the ball was at the exact right spot, and there was a crash of sound that you know is perfect before you even see the ball heading out, out and—there is always a pause before—it's over the fence for a grand slam home run. Can you imagine that?

The picture of the cop, without his hat, with his 9mm pistol safely tucked in its holster, looking and acting like the cop on the beat and being part of his community was the exact right moment in exactly the right place. His name is Mel. I did not ask last names, because guys and gals standing by a fence watching a game are not formal. They only use first names.

He said he hoped he would not get in hot water for this. I told him, and then said on air, that he had done more good for the image of the entire police department than a stack of press releases from their public relations people.

It was a very good game.

How to Treat the Media ... or Anyone

Politicians have a direct way of dealing with problems. They hide. Heads of corporations do the same. The police, sometimes. Little kids, always. Etc., etc., and ...

Etc. That means so many use this tactic that you might think not answering is the preferred way of answering a question.

You can understand little kids not answering. If they say something wrong they might get spanked. Or sent to their room. Or, worse, denied a video game. Those are real punishments.

I am talking about not answering to the media, where there is no punishment. And please do not think that the media is one organization and it ought to keep its nose out of other people's business. The media is *you*. When you read a newspaper or watch the TV news and someone is not answering a question about something, they are not answering *you*. They are avoiding *you*. And that is a bummer.

I recently found the baseball guide to dealing with the media. It was put out by the New York Yankees, whom I now suddenly admire because of this.

After many incidents when players would swing a fist at the media, and therefore look like they were less than loveable, management came up with this brief outline. It has only four points, like four bases, like baseball.

Be accessible, be honest, be humble and be accountable.

Oh, my gosh. Would those not be the best qualities that you could hope for in a politician?

And I would add a few tips about what to do when actually speaking with reporters, or anyone—and one bit of super-practical advice:

1) Think before you speak. There are no do-overs.

2) Nothing is ever off the record.

3) Lies beget lies and bending the truth will ultimately find its way back to you.

4) Do not under any circumstances take a naked picture of yourself and send it to anyone. With Twitter and email and other forms of social media, anything you do that is stupid will spread like fire in a fireworks factory.

But would it not be good for a politician, or a neighbour or a co-worker or yourself to follow the first three rules? No more would you hear "I did not say that. I was misquoted. I was taken out of context. I would never say that. And if I did say that I did not mean to say that. What I meant to say was not what you heard me say. The media is at fault."

It Is So Good to Be Home

It is the first thing you say when you walk in the door. It may be a small apartment at the top of a long elevator ride, but when you walk into your home you feel at home.

Obviously you feel that way—it is your home—but that feeling is more than just the fact of being at home. It may be a row house in a boring row of houses but when you get home from work you feel better when you walk through the door. That is not boring.

You know this, I know this. Going back to the old neighbourhood, too, has an excitement that you cannot explain. You see the old houses, the old trees and the old telephone poles and you remember when they and you made one world—yours. If friends are with you they don't see what you see. It is a mystery of life that we live in our own worlds.

So I ask you, why do I keep looking for something new?

I was riding around town with Dave McKay. I have told you about him before. He is a barbecue chef who is a news cameraman only because it supports his barbecue habit. He is very good at taking pictures. He is very, very good at smoking pork butts.

He was telling me about the briskets he had made the day before. That's beef, not pork. I wasn't listening. As soon as he mentioned briskets I went back to my world, when I was a teenager and worked in a meat-packing house in Brooklyn.

Down in the basement, below the floor where the rest of the meat was being cut and packaged, one happy butcher sat alone at a table next to a sink. He had a rubber tube attached to the faucet and at the other end of the tube was a hypodermic needle.

He also had a stack of beef briskets.

He would put one of them on a scale in front of him, insert the needle and push a small lever with his thumb. Water squirted into the brisket. He was a good butcher. He knew where to put the needle so the water would not leak out.

Then he watched the scale move up. Four, five ounces. Enough. He moved the needle to another part of the meat. Squirt. Four, five more ounces. Eight, nine, ten ounces, in total, more than a third of a pound in a five-pound brisket. Not a bad profit for water.

That was all I knew about briskets.

Dave and I were in Stanley Park and I could see a huge cruise ship in port. It might have been the first of the year.

"How about that?"

"The guy jogging with the red shorts and green shirt?"

"No, the ship with white sides and white smoke stacks."

"I thought you were colour blind," he said.

"That's why I saw the ship."

We drove back to the convention centre where the ship was docked, and all the way there I kept saying this will be easy.

We will find someone getting off the ship and they will tell us the exciting new things they hope to see in Vancouver. Or if we are late we might find someone coming back to the ship and they will tell us the exciting new things they have just seen.

We can't lose.

The first couple we met were English, from Winnipeg. That makes sense. They loved our transit system.

That's nice, I thought.

Then a Chinese woman from California. She thought Stanley Park was beautiful.

Nice, I thought. And I am getting worried. They sound like a government press release.

Next was the red-haired son of a woman from Boston who told us he and his mother had been to Granville Island, but she spent most of her time in an earring store. That is both funny and sad, and it lets you know what really happens on many trips. From the boat or the plane to the stores and the malls. We have to buy something to bring back to someone who was not there from a place that was not seen.

And then, there they were—two fellows who looked contented. Two fellows not dressed in new touring clothes. They were clean and neat, but their clothes were worn. They each held an overstuffed plastic shopping bag.

"You are crew members?" I asked.

Yes.

"Where are you from, if I may ask?"

"The Philippines."

Most of the crew is Filipino, especially the ones working below decks who keep the ship sailing.

"Do you go sightseeing?" I asked.

Sometimes, they said, but mostly they work whether they are docked or on the water.

"How long have you been away from home?"

"Eight months," one said.

"Long time," I said.

"Not long now," the other one said. He lifted his plastic bag.

"What do you have? Where did you go?" All the quick questions.

"Junk food, Filipino junk food," they both said.

They opened their bags. It looked like potato chips. "Fried pig skin," said one of them, and his face brightened like he had just stepped through the doorway of his home.

"Miss it?" I asked the obvious.

"More than 100 percent," he said.

During their two hours of free time they had been straight to a Filipino grocery store. No park, no museum, no statues could come close to going home, even if it was only fried pig skin.

The Dribbler

Zen was big when the hippies discovered it. Of course Zen had been around for centuries, but when the hippies learned to spell it everything was Zen.

"Can you feel it?"

"I can feel your vibes, man. Do you feel mine?"

"Your vibes are my vibes. We are at peace with the inner self."

And then they smoked some more pot.

Once you discover something, it is yours and you become the first person on earth to know about it.

"You are not still doing yoga, are you? That is so passé. I'm into Pilates, with my own personal Pilates instructor."

"My personal instructor is into weight training. He says Pilates only makes you *think* you are getting stronger."

Every week there is a new way to get a new body and mind.

And then there was the basketball. Thump, thump. And it kept going. Thump. Thump. One fellow alone on the basketball court, dribbling. He is there every day, except in really bad weather. He dribbles, sometimes slow, sometimes a little faster, and sometimes a little fancy, slowly passing the ball from hand to hand around his back.

"You could call it basketball yoga, or ball chi," he said.

He laughed. Without putting down yoga or tai chi he said this was what he did.

But he really didn't care what you call it. He called it bouncing his basketball.

His name is Omar Cetiner, and during the off-season from fall 'til spring you can find him on one of the four empty courts at Kitsilano Beach. They are empty because the Park Board in its lack of wisdom takes down the hoops after the summer.

They do this because residents across the street complained that young people were playing there during the winter and, after a summer of games, the residents should have some peace. So young people cannot play and the residents do not complain. Apparently young people should go away and play somewhere else.

But this is the way it is and it is good for Omar. He dribbles. Even if there were baskets on the backboards he would not shoot at them.

"Then it gets competitive," he said. "And I am here for the bouncing."

He bounces his basketball for an hour or so a day and in that time he is exercising, dancing and meditating. He gets to be at peace with himself, he thinks about things and solves problems, and then, he said, he realizes he doesn't have problems.

That's not bad for a basketball. In the past two years he has lost twenty-five pounds, which is only a pound a month but that means he will never gain it back.

"I used to kick a soccer ball around. That was the same," he said.

He did not worry about the right way to kick or to bounce. He kicked gently, and he bounces the same. He does not worry about what to call it. He does not tell others to do this. He does not pay for lessons.

And when I asked, stupidly, if he invented this way of exercising he said of course not. "It's only bouncing a ball. It is my Zen. It is a dance with the ball." And then he went on bouncing.

But the best thing was he didn't even once say I should try it.

The Ironworkers Photo

There is one picture taken long ago that takes everyone's breath away.

I saw it when I was growing up, I saw it in a hundred card shops. You have seen it, too.

I last saw it while interviewing a man who was giving a fishing rod and reel to his son. The father had just stopped at a junk shop on Main Street and saw something he thought his son would like. He didn't know it was the perfect gift.

Back to the fishing rod. Stories bounce around, like life. Were it not for the fishing rod, I would not have stopped him to ask why he was carrying one on Main Street, where there are no fish.

He said it was for his son who wanted a rod for his girlfriend to go fishing. The man, Harry Down, said the rod was something he'd picked up at Canadian Tire a few years ago, but the reel was special. It was a Mitchell 300, made in France. He got it when he was ten years old. He is now fifty-eight. Now it was a gift for his son. That is beautiful.

That was enough of a story for me.

But what is in the bag, if we may ask? We ask everything. No one has to answer, but if you ask things in life, life gets better.

He opened a plastic bag and took out a picture. No, impossible, it was *the* picture. You are going to see it now in your memory. It is of a row of men sitting on a steel girder about seventy stories above the ground. They are having lunch. They are talking with each other. They are lighting cigarettes. They are oblivious to the clear, visible, unavoidable fact that if they lean too far forward or back they will fall to their death.

Before they died there would be a long, long, and even longer, scream. Then thud. And the scream would be silent. Then the others would go back to work. Look it up on the internet right now. Look up Rockefeller Center construction photos. It will be one of the first pictures that comes up. Hold your breath.

There are eleven men sitting on the girder, but they are so comfortable that it defies logic or belief. They look like they are just having their lunch break. Many people cannot look at the picture. I am one of them, but I am mesmerized by it. When I do see it in the window of a photo store, in a history book or as a postcard I cannot take my eyes off it. When you see it you won't be able to either. Try it.

It was a posed photo. Just for the fun of it they were asked to walk out on that beam and pretend they were having lunch so the photographer could get a snap. They did. There are no safety harnesses or ropes or hard hats or steel-toed boots. Of course hats and boots wouldn't do you much good flying down at 160 clicks an hour. The trip would take less than ten seconds.

The photographer was just after a quirky idea and said to some guys, go risk your lives for me. And they did.

If you are afraid of heights you will get stomach jitters. You will not be able to look. Then you will look again. Then you will close your eyes. Then you will dream about it.

Anyway, back to the story. Harry bought this for his son who was graduating from BCIT's Ironworkers program. I saw the picture and said, "Wow, that is the world's most classic ironworkers photo."

Harry said he didn't know that. I told him it was taken at the top of the Rockefeller Center, the place where the TV show *30 Rock* takes place. He said he didn't know that.

Then he saw his son and gave him the fishing rod and reel.

"Thanks," said his son.

And then he gave him the picture.

"Wow. Oh, wow!"

His son stared at it. He smiled. He looked. He loved it.

"Do you know where it was taken?" his father asked.

"The Empire State Building?" said his son, whose name is Lance.

"No," said his father. "It was the top of the Rockefeller Center in New York."

Sometimes fathers are so smart.

It really did not matter whether Lance understood what the Rockefeller Center was. His father had told him and that was all that mattered.

Then Lance said, "Thanks, Dad," and gave him a hug.

And the cameraman, Tony Clark, saw the other perfect picture. You have to be a good photographer to see the perfect picture.

Harry's eyes were wet, and he was trying to hide that from Lance. He moved his head away, but the camera stayed on his eyes, and the tears came and then Lance hugged him, again. This time it was a deep and long hug. And what Harry did was try to hide his eyes behind his son's shoulder.

What is the point of all this? One thing always leads to another. A photographer in the depression wanted to get a quirky picture to make people smile. Eighty years later it brought a tear to a father's eye.

Never discount the little guy. Never discount how one picture that makes you think about someone else is almost always the perfect gift.

The '57 Chevy

had just dropped off my wife at a bus stop to go to work and was
driving back to meet a cameraman when I saw it in a gas station.

Blue. With fins. Old. Boxy. Round. How did they make it round
and boxy at the same time? It must have been magic.

A 1957 Chevy.

Oh. My gosh. You've probably noticed how many stories begin
with Oh. My gosh. That is the salt and pepper on a steak. Oh, my
gosh, this is going to taste good for my memory.

Almost all of us have a favourite woman or man. That has been
going on since we crawled out of the ooze and became people. Maybe
it happened before then. The people we remember, sometimes in secret, are the most important.

And we have a favourite food. The Roman soldiers said, "That
bread we had last night was the best ever." The ancient Jews said, "My,

that bread was really good." And before them the ancient Greeks said, "Never have I tasted such good bread."

Bread has been around for a long time. It is funny that since the Last Supper of Jesus, the Christians have come to greatly honour the bread and wine. Jesus told his friends that every time you eat bread and drink wine you should think about him. So in churches around the world the bread and wine became holy objects. That is odd. When Jesus was breaking the bread it was basically the only thing they had for breakfast, lunch and dinner. Bread was the main, and usually only, food. Sometimes they got a fig or a couple of olives thrown in. And if they lived near the ocean they got a fish occasionally. And maybe once or twice a year some lamb. But for Sunday dinner it was bread.

The same with wine. They drank wine a dozen times a day. They drank only wine. They could not drink the water—it would make them sick—but they learned that if they mixed water in with wine they could drink it and stay alive, which was a good choice. Babies drank wine. Holy folks drank wine. Everyone drank wine and ate bread, and that was basically it until the big feast days, when they added a sliver of meat.

If Jesus was around today, heaven help him, he would have told his friends whenever you have a Starbucks and a burger, think of me. I know this sounds irreligious, but there is no disrespect meant. It's just an attempt to put the image into perspective.

What we do on a daily basis is drink coffee and eat hamburgers, or bagels. It would be the same thing as bread and wine back then. The foods we remember, often for oddball reasons, are the most important.

So anyway, pardon the detour, but your best meal has more history to it than your best car. However, after your Lord, your lover and your lunch, your best car comes very close.

Mine was a '57 Chevy.

Some men are now thinking of their '57 Chevys. It was not like other cars. Modern cars are like other cars. Now all cars are basically the same, but not in 1957.

The back fenders were like shark fins. The engine was as quiet as a shark. The zoom zoom was remarkable for a hunk of dead-weight steel that was three times heavier than any car on the road today, and it was as swift as a shark. It is hard to get a heavy weight to move, but the '57 Chevy did it.

I needed a car. I was living in a shack off a United States Air Force base in Florida. I was living with my wife and child. I had to get to the base in the morning, and I was hitchhiking. It is hard to thumb a ride at 6 a.m.

"Here's a nice car for you," my sergeant said. "A '57 Chevy."

I had no idea what it meant. I had never driven a car before. I grew up, as you probably know, in New York, and even though the streets were filled with cars, no one had a car. I have, or had, relatives in New York in their sixties and seventies who never sat behind the wheel of a car. You take the subway or a taxi.

"Here's the car, kid," the owner said to me.

The nose was in a blackberry bramble. I got in. There was no Drive, Neutral or Reverse. There was just a stick.

I got out. I was embarrassed. I had given the nice man $150 but I couldn't drive it.

The sergeant and his friend laughed—at me. That is not good. The sergeant got in and backed it out. Then he showed me how the gears worked.

The car had no floor. It had rotted away in the salt of the ground and the salt of the air.

I put in some sheet metal and patched the holes.

A little while later I had my infant daughter on the front seat after taking my wife somewhere. My daughter was wrapped up in the things you wrap babies in. Someone in front of me stopped suddenly and I jammed my foot down on the brakes. My daughter flew off the seat, hit the firewall in front and shot up under the dashboard, and got stuck there.

The car in front moved forward and as I drove on I reached down, taking my eyes off the road, grabbed at the blanket around her and pulled her down. Then I dropped her back on the seat and drove home.

Two hours later I drove back and picked up my wife. (I never told her what happened. I still haven't. If she reads this she will not speak to me for a while. And then she will say things in an unkind manner.) On our way home we stopped for coffee and burgers, and now every time I have coffee and a burger I think of that car.

I did a story on television, of course, about the '57 Chevy that I saw on Renfrew Street in Vancouver. I never mentioned my car or my daughter or the hole in the floor or the burgers and coffee.

It is not the '57 Chevy that counts. Just like with your first car, you remember that back seat, or you remember your kids or your speeding ticket or the breakdown on a lonely highway. It is not the car. It went to the junkyard long ago. It is you and that car and that memory that keep chugging along. You are the important thing in the picture. Without you that '57 Chevy would have gone nowhere.

As much as we love the old things, we should love our old self, too. Look in a mirror and say, "You look pretty good. You are kind of a classic. You remind me of the best times of all."

And then drive yourself around the block and think what a lucky person you are to have you. After that, climb in the back seat and remember some other things, like the best times of all.

The Odyssey of a Dodge

The end of the story was just the beginning. We were driving along Second Avenue when I saw a For Sale sign on an old car. A very old car. And not just old, but the kind of old car no one would want.

I had no idea what it was, but it was black and plain and boring. It was not an old Chevy or Ford. They are in demand by folks who like to restore cars. It was not the basis of a hot rod, which are seldom made any longer. It was not sexy or curvaceous. It was boring.

"It's a Dodge," said Al Cronheimer, a mechanic who loves old cars.

It belonged to a friend who was not there. Darn. But he would call him and get him back. Wonderful. Emotions are just a call away.

Meanwhile, Al told me the six-cylinder 1950 engine was also used to power welding shops and lathes and all sorts of industrial jobs as well as running the Dodge. It was not souped up, it was just an old, hard-working motor.

The car was a bit bashed in on the hood and there were dents under the headlights and more dents around the front fenders. It looked like it had taken a beating.

"But it still runs," he said. "And it will probably run for years. It's just a simple car that works."

The For Sale sign on the windshield said, "Runs Fantastic." Sure, I thought. And so does my old lawnmower, the one with no wheels.

But even with the sign, no one wanted to buy it. It had been on the used car lot for well over a year now and no one had even asked about it.

The owner and his friend returned. They had been picking up car parts. That's what people who fix cars do when they are not fixing cars. The two of them looked like Al. They had blue jeans and loose-fitting heavy shirts and smiles and hands outstretched to shake. You cannot beat a smile for a greeting.

Good greetings can sometimes be a good story on their own. And usually a good greeting means that something is coming right after it.

"You want a good story?" asked Sandy Flett, who also loves old cars.

See, just like I said.

"A tow-truck driver dropped it off one day. He said the owner and his wife had a falling out and she took a hammer to his car."

It was a new wife and an old car that he insisted on keeping. It is strange the things that can get us upset.

"She had bashed in the headlights, the parking lights and fenders, and knocked off the hood ornament," said Sandy.

Then she called the tow truck to take it away.

"In one day he lost his wife and his car."

The speculation was that she wanted something newer, and he did not. This old and faithful car would cost nothing to run, which would please him. On the other hand it looked like an old car and not even a fancy old car, just an old car, and that would not please her.

That would lead to other things, like the price of eggs or savings accounts or how much was spent on this or even that. And that would lead to an argument and then things would get worse.

That is the only thing for a fact. Things got very much worse.

Goodbye marriage. Goodbye car.

And then it was taken to a place of love, at least car love.

"I fixed the fenders and headlights and parking lights," said Sandy. "And I have the hood ornament ready to go back on."

Things go bad, and then things can be fixed if you work on them. It is a very simple rule of life.

Sandy and his friend Vern Bethel sat on the front fenders talking and laughing about the car. I have done stories on Vern. He fixes classic cars like Bentleys and Rolls Royces. He, like his friends, breathes and lives cars.

"The sign is true," Vern said. "It really does run fantastic, and it will keep on going for a long time. It just doesn't look very fancy."

That is another rule in life. It doesn't have to be explained.

Neighbourhood Parade

There is nothing, absolutely nothing, better than watching a parade—unless you are in a parade.

My neighbourhood has a yearly parade. It was started by someone with a lot of heart and the stomach to get something going when nothing was going before.

But now it is established, it is a tradition, and on a Sunday in the middle of June many people with many more kids gather at the end of the street. There is a marching band from a local school, and some politicians who get in their cars and throw candy to the kids. There is also a fire truck and some police, or at least auxiliary police, to make sure it looks like there are police there in case something bad happens, although nothing bad has ever happened.

The only strange thing about this parade is that almost no one has ever seen it.

Some of the kids are on bicycles, and some parents or kids have costumes. Sometimes there is a theme, like the old west or fairy tales, and the kids dress up. But most times folks just show up.

My neighbours once organized a lawnmower drill team, which was extra special. Four of them pushed their mowers in somewhat planned drill team directions. Sometimes they looked good, and sometimes they crashed. But you can't beat a drill team walking down a street while others behind them are trying to go around them because the mowers are holding up the parade.

But again, almost no one was watching.

The problem is everyone wants to be in the parade.

Sometimes there is a new family and they have heard about this parade and they come out to the street with their chairs and coffee and sit down and say, "This must be the wrong day. No one is on the street waiting."

And then they hear the band coming and they say, "This must really be a very bad parade. No one is here to watch. I think we should go inside before someone sees us waiting to watch something that no one wants to see."

Included in this little family is a small girl. She has been waiting for the parade because she knows parades are fun, like the Santa Parade downtown. But downtown the streets are packed with people, so many that she can hardly see the parade.

This is different. There is no one in front of her. She can hear the band, but there is no one beside her. Now she can just see the fire truck that is leading the parade, but there is nobody else to share this moment.

And then the truck passes and the firemen wave at her and her parents. "All of this just for me?" she thinks.

And then the band comes and it is fun. But she and her parents are alone. She smiles. She applauds. Her parents are looking to see if anyone else has come out. Look there. There is someone across the street who has just walked to the curb. One person. They are not alone. But one person and all this music?

And then the people in the parade walk by. Hundreds of them, some in costume, some on bikes or trikes or in wagons, some in baby carriages, some with dogs, come walking past the little girl.

She waves. They wave back.

Then the politicians come. They are in cars and they are waving. Wait, one is walking, but she is walking in front of the car that has her name across it. Politicians are funny people. They want you to know who they are, they just don't want you to know what they do.

And then more kids, but this time it is a few from her class. "Look Mommy, there's Kate and there's Alice. And there is Jas. And they are waving at us."

The kids are motioning her to join them. "Can I Mommy, can I?"

Her mother is not sure of the protocol but one of the kids in the parade runs over to the sidewalk and grabs the hand of the little girl and pulls her into the parade. Her mother, who has been worrying about her daughter making friends, feels her eyes getting wet.

She steps off the curb and starts walking behind her daughter. Someone says hello to her.

That is two less people watching.

A very elderly couple are by their door watching. They have spent years walking, now it is their time to watch.

In total, over the six blocks that the parade goes from where it starts to the end at the local school, there are about twenty people watching. But there are now countless people walking. By the time it reaches the halfway point there are no viewers. Everyone has stepped off the sidewalk and joined the multitude.

At the end there is a small carnival with some home-baked cupcakes for sale and a few arts and crafts tables. But the purpose of the parade is the parade.

It happens in North Vancouver, but that does not matter. It could happen anywhere. You just have to find someone who has the heart and stomach to say to his neighbours, why don't we have a parade? We could get people together just to walk down the street and maybe someone can play the kazoo or something and we could celebrate having neighbours?

What do you think?

Remember, there is nothing better than watching a parade, except being in one. You could make your own, and you will not have to worry about crowd control.

Sailing Down the River

The last time I wrote about this it was in a park and that reminded me of a street a long time ago. The next time I wrote about it, it was in a street, and that reminded someone else of a long time ago.

Sadly, it is something else that has disappeared: sailing sticks down the gutter in the street.

We were driving up or down Victoria Drive when suddenly, gush. It looked like a car had hit a fire hydrant and there was a tower of white bubbly water surging up higher than the head of the guy with a reflective vest and waterproof hip waders who was watching it.

This is nice. It must be done on purpose, because why else would he have been prepared with the right clothing for a gushing tower? Plus there was a sign that said Street Closed and there were a few portable orange barriers around the puddle that covered half the corner. Also there was no car smashed into anything. Perfect for stopping and taking pictures.

And one of the nicest things about it was that the fellow in the hip waders was pleasant. His name was Kyle Navayan and he told us he was cleaning the line that brings fresh water to homes in the area. He opened up the hydrant and out came the water and residue while he tested and retested until the water in the test was sparkling. It is good to know this is done occasionally. It makes the water we drink taste better.

But look at all this opportunity shooting up in the air and flowing down the street. It was an instant playground. It was a place to stomp and splash. It was something to watch and wonder about nature coming out of a steel stump and covering an asphalt street.

It was also in the way. One grumpy fellow wanted to cross the street and looked quite displeased that the puddle was in his way. He said an impolite word and walked around it.

But then a young mother with two little ones in a stroller pushed them right through the shallow edge of the water with a loud "Weeeee." Now that is the kind of mother to have. Plus she was smart enough to push with an outstretched arm holding the stroller and her feet skirting the flood. The wheels got wet, she stayed dry and the kids had fun.

She turned the stroller around, pointed the mesmerized faces at the gusher and told them it was water, and some little sparks of excitement ignited in their brains and their lives would be ever so slightly better for this moment.

Another woman whipped around the puddle on her bike, because if her tires got wet it could be dangerous or, worse, the water could have been thrown up on her clothes. This is not like the kid who goes through the deepest part with legs held up and then suddenly realizes that, without peddling, the water will slow down the bike to a stop and then the bike will tilt to one side, where there's nothing but water, or to the other side, where there is also nothing but water, and suddenly—oh, you know the rest. You were there, long ago.

And then Kyle said the water was fine and shut off the hydrant and moved on to make another instant playground. He took away his signs and drove off. The story was over. The large puddle was shrinking with the water flowing downhill as all the creeks that were once here once did. But this little stream had only half a block to go before it went into a sewer.

And then came that great moment when memory took over and replaced disappointment. I picked up a dried leaf and dropped it into the water. It shot off. It didn't drift gently away, it zoomed. The water was moving fast and the leaf was as light as a ... leaf. It hit the back of a tire that was holding up a car and bounced off, and then rippled over some rapids caused by sand or pebbles hidden deep beneath the running river.

When you set sail on fast-moving water you never know what dangers you might run into. A pop bottle could be right there, right in your way as you fly down the river and you cannot do anything but hold on and hope that the current pulls you around it. You could get stuck right under a tire and there is no way out. You are doomed.

I put another leaf in and rode on it with water splashing on my face and then the boat spun around and I was going backwards. Now that is scary and exciting. And then down the sewer, but of course I jumped off before the unforgiving end.

The leaf sailing off in the sparkling sunlight that slipped between the parked cars was the last picture in the story. And then back to the anchors.

"I remember when I used to do that. I had forgotten all about it," said Wayne Cox. He had the smile of someone who had been on some wild boat rides along a curb long ago.

That was the high point of the story. It was after the story was over that he said he remembered. It was a high point because he had that memory, and a low point, because so many kids now have never sailed a leaf or a stick down the gutter.

I know this is true. Of course you are going to say you did it, and yes, you did and I am glad, but I spend every day of my working and not working life on the street looking for things, as you know. I am out in the rain, I am out after school and on weekends, and I just don't see it anymore.

The gutter navy once enrolled almost every kid between the ages of about five and ten. When it rained you put popsicle sticks or twigs or even little boats made of folded paper into the water at the edge of the curb and watched them go. Sometimes you would run alongside, sometimes you just kept launching ships until you had a convoy. The rain would run down the back of your coat but you couldn't pull into port because there was a mission to finish or a race or a war or peace going on. There was always something on the water and you were the captain.

I saw some kids doing this in a park ten years ago. They were having so much fun. It wasn't a gutter, but a real stream with grass on both sides, but that didn't bother them, except when a kid slipped on the grass and fell in. Still they went on sailing. There was a father with them, which is good and which is always the case now. I don't know if he had suggested they sail their sticks or if they thought of it, but that doesn't matter. The fact is they did it. It's also a fact that I haven't seen others doing it since then. I know some are there, I just haven't seen them. At least, I hope they are there.

When I saw those kids in the park it reminded me of when I was in the gutter navy and we had great wars on our street with sailors from other navies doing nasty things, as happens in wars. There was kicking of boats and hurling of rocks and building of dams to deflect the destroyers out into the street to be run over by passing cars. We did not fool around when it came to battles on the ocean.

Now it is too dangerous to let kids play by themselves next to the street, and unless they are at soccer practice they are not allowed to stay out in the rain, which is the only time the tide is high.

But Wayne remembered, and that was at the same moment thousands, tens of thousands, of you remembered.

Maybe, just maybe, the next time it rains would be a good time to sign up a recruit for a ship that is ready to take off for some distant port. You were once the captain. You never forget.

So Big

The funniest thing about the story of the man from Spain riding his motorcycle around the world was his cup of coffee.

"I asked for a small cup," he said in his video of his travels.

He held up a cup that would hold twenty espressos. It was probably a Tall in Starbucks' talk. You ask for a small and they hear tall and give you a cup that, in Spanish terms, is like filling the swimming pool to take a bath.

Not so long ago coffee cups were shaped like coffee cups, small with a gently sloping side. They held four ounces of coffee, four and a half if you filled it to the brim. That was what you had with breakfast, and another one in the afternoon during a break, and another one after dinner. I still have one of the cups I stole from a US Air Force mess hall.

We thought we drank a lot of coffee.

Then came the mugs, which would hold two of the old-fashioned cups. Then came the Starbucks' Tall, which sounds like Small and holds twelve ounces, which is three of the old-fashioned cups.

But that was not enough because next came the Grande, the Italian name for large. That holds sixteen ounces. And you had two, oh, let's stop again, three of them a day.

Then came Venti, the Italian name for twenty because it holds twenty-four ounces (which makes perfect sense).

I am not knocking Starbucks at all. I wish I had thought of a way to sell a legal drug that makes you feel good and makes you come back for more day after day, or even hour after hour.

I am not even mocking the super size of the drinks. It is just that one Venti is more than anyone whom I served with in the Air Force would drink in an entire day, even if they were heavy coffee drinkers.

"You don't mean you had *five* cups of coffee today? You must be a nervous wreck." That was still one cup less than a single Venti.

But there are Venti drinkers who cannot go for a walk from shop to office without a cup in their hand, and they go back again for lunch and, oh, maybe cut down to just a Grande after work.

And most of the coffees, not all but most of the coffees, have sugar in them. It is put in by the customers because it tastes good. No argument.

It doesn't matter how much sugar is added, one spoon, two, or just pour it in. It doesn't matter because who is counting?

This all goes along with the super-sized soft drinks that are all sugar, and I read a story in the *New York Times* about the mayor of that city wanting to ban those. The story asked if the rule would apply to super-big coffees, which are all the rage. The *Times* reporter referred to them as catnip for coffee drinkers and called them coffee milk shakes.

Back to the motorcycle fellow from Spain with his small coffee that wasn't small at all. In Spain someone was watching his video on the internet. That someone was having a coffee. It was in a small cup, with a tiny bit of sugar.

It was one ounce.

That's it. That is the entire punch line. And you look at all the people who are large and wonder how did this happen? We have no idea.

Just one other thing. My wife asked me to get some sugar at the supermarket last week. I got the two-kilogram bag. That is five pounds.

When I was young and went to the store to get sugar, the five-pound bag was the largest that was sold. Now it is the smallest.

Steve Jobs May Have Saved the World

His influence was profound. I see it all around me. You see it too.
Steve Jobs, the incredible genius behind the Macintosh computer and the iPhone and the iPad reshaped the world.

Yes, of course, everyone knows that. He invented something you can hold in your hand and use to do just about anything except sweep the floors. And soon there will be an app for that.

But there is something else that has nothing to do with computers and has everything to do with the fact Steve Jobs was skinny. Whatever body fat ratio means, which I don't know, Steve Jobs must have had zero. There was no fat under his skin, just bones and ideas.

Because he was smart and worked hard and invented new stuff he became rich and famous, and that is what almost everyone wants. And if you can't be what you want, at least you can look like someone who is what he or she wants to be.

When the Beatles crossed the Atlantic in the early 1960s, all the boys in Canada and America had crewcuts. The Beatles had long hair. Actually it was just down to their ears, but that was long back then. Along came the Beatles and the crewcuts of a pair of nations disappeared. Within five years all boys, except the ones who were in favour of the war and against civil rights along with hating the Beatles, had long hair.

After the 1970s miniskirts had grown longer and were almost reaching the knees. Thirty years later the women in *Sex and the City* slipped them up their well-exercised legs, and skirts around the world followed in the same direction.

We just simply like looking like those whom we like. There is nothing strange or inhuman about that. And Steve Jobs was skinny. He was skinny in a world growing fat.

Now, wherever you are, go to the Wall Street area of your city and narrow your vision. The men will be skinny. Somehow or other they have lost gobs of poundage almost overnight in their pursuit of looking like the founder of Apple.

This is a good thing, because first the investment people, then the computer people and then the rest of us will want to look like everyone else who is getting rich and potentially famous.

This wish to be like those we admire does not extend to the way others think or act. It usually stops at the way they dress or walk, and sometimes the way they eat.

We who follow the herd are not profound thinkers, but at least the current leader of the pack had a physique we could all do better carrying. If we became like Steve Jobs we would be healthier, which is something we would not have to buy or download or worry about updating. And if we use a laptop we might have enough room left on our lap to put it.

Terry Keeps on Running

It was raining. It rained a lot on Terry when he was running. That would have been squish, his left good foot hitting the highway, then kunk, his right foot of plastic and metal hitting the same ground.

The water squirted out under his left foot because all the weight of his lean body was on that one. The water sort of fluttered out from under his right foot because he more or less hopped on that one.

He was hopping across Canada. We all said he was running, but he was really hopping, one big push with his left, one hop with his arms going up when his right hit the ground.

That was in 1980, a long time ago.

He brought together the country more than any other Canadian has ever done, either before or since. I have written about him in an earlier book, you know. I said a statue of him should be over the Parliament Buildings in Ottawa so all the leaders of the country could

250

look up as they went to work on the problems of the country and they would know what to do when they got inside.

They would stop bickering and posturing and lapdogging and get the job done.

You also know that I was the last reporter to talk to him. It was not a formal, quick interview. I spent hours with him and we talked of many things—God, sports, friends, family, Canada. His only wish was that he could get out of bed and go back on his run.

He couldn't. He died in that bed. He was a month away from his twenty-third birthday.

And that was a long time ago. Thirty-one years later, on a rainy day in the spring of 2012, I was looking at the new Terry Fox Memorial next to the stadium with the new roof. It is a beautiful statue. It is actually four statues, like four freeze-frames of him growing steadily larger as he runs toward you with that so distinctive gait, just like his last wish.

It was made by Douglas Coupland, a writer and artist in Vancouver who writes about Generation X, which not many understand, and he makes statues that everyone understands.

As I said, it was raining. No one was in the plaza where the statue is. Why would you stand there getting wet?

And then three people who *were* getting wet—a little girl and two women—stopped in front of the first image of Terry. The two women were listening to the little girl. She pointed at his leg, then spoke to them, then pointed again.

The rain came down, but they ignored it. They did not have umbrellas.

I moved as close as I could without trying to look like I was listening and I listened. There was not a word I could understand.

"Excuse me," I said, because I had to. You don't let life's moments pass without joining them.

"Where are you from, if I may ask?"

One of the women said Afghanistan.

How could this be? Canadian soldiers are in Afghanistan fighting or keeping the peace or both. They are certainly dying there. Are there immigrants here from a country that is battling against us? Well, yes, and that makes this country something special.

"We are learning about Terry Fox from her," one of the women said. She gestured to the little one.

"She learned about him in preschool and we wanted to see the statue."

She was five years old. She was teaching her mother, who doesn't speak any English, and her aunt, who does, about a country's strange hero who carried no weapons and fought only pain and disease.

"Does the rain bother you?" I asked.

"She told us Terry Fox ran in the rain and the sun," the aunt said.

I asked them a few more things, when they came to Canada and why. They came because this is a good country, the aunt said, and it was about three years ago. But during this brief conversation we had blinked and hadn't noticed that little one had slipped away.

In a panic that was instant the mother looked around and called her name in her language, which is really the universal language of mothers. "Please, where are you? Please be here. Do not be gone."

And then we saw her. She had moved back to the smallest statue, still much bigger than her but more her size than the large sculpture we were standing next to. She had wrapped one of her arms around Terry's artificial leg and was looking up at him.

You know those images you never forget? That was one of them.

They called her and she came and said goodbye to me. But as they were leaving the mother, who did not speak English, said in English, "I want strong to be." Then there was a long pause, "Like Terry Fox."

When she gets her citizenship papers she will be a good citizen of this country, even though she is from a country where soldiers from this country have died. In her life, Terry has just started running again.

They left and the rain kept coming down. No one else showed up, at least not while I was there. It was just the statue with the water sliding down from Terry's face and the three from Afghanistan walking away.

The rain has a great deal of connection with that day, because out by the sidewalk they stopped, turned around and looked at the statue again. Little one pointed back at it and told them something more. They nodded and stared silently with the water coming down on their heads.

That was like Terry, ignoring the rain, going one step further. The woman who wanted to be strong already was.

The Special Driver

I know you thought there was a special lane for you, just you. We all know you always have your special lane, because you are special.

It was snowing this morning, heavy, wet snow, and on Highway 1 just north of the Second Narrows Bridge the road goes up at a breathtaking incline that's difficult to drive in the snow.

There were many cars lined up to get onto the highway, but we were creeping slowly, so slowly that we can understand why you needed your special lane. We were creeping because the hill we were facing was covered with wet, slippery snow and everyone was going at creeping speed.

And then you came past us in your special lane. You were going faster than us because there was no one in front of you, because none of us are special. We are just ordinary schmucks who creep along waiting for our turn to crawl up the hill.

You went past all those cars and we watched, and watched, and thought, Gee, you must be special and we are not.

But then your special lane ended and apparently you didn't notice, because suddenly you were off the edge of the road and you were trying to drive on the grass and mud that was covered with snow and ice. You probably saw us waving at you as we crept by while your wheels were spinning.

That was a very special moment for the rest of us.

The Special Driver, Part Two

That previous story was a heart-warming moment on a cold day for many of us. But sometimes you see the wrong turned right when you are alone.

On First Avenue and Manitoba Street there was a policeman in a police car stuck behind a tiny BobCat. A BobCat, as you know is the humble runt of the tractor family. It doesn't take up much room and it does a good job, but it does not go very fast.

The policeman did not have on his flashing red emergency lights, so he is supposed to drive like the rest of us, with patience and following the rules. But we know he was special because there was only one way to get around the little BobCat. He drove up onto the median in the middle of the road. That is also called a Traffic Island, the purpose of which is to create a sanctuary away from traffic. There were no people on the island now, or I am sure the nice policeman would not have driven up there.

Anyway, the policeman did get around the BobCat, drove down off the curb of the island back onto the road in front of the BobCat and scooted ahead. Then a moment later was stopped by a red light. He stopped for the red light because he had no emergency lights on, so he is, you know, supposed to drive like the rest of us.

But that pesky little BobCat kept coming. In just a moment he would be stopped by the same red light that was stopping the nice policeman. Of course, the nice policeman could see him coming in his mirror. He knew what the driver of the BobCat would be doing. He knew he would be smiling because that is what you do when someone passes you on a traffic island and then gets stuck behind a red light. You smile and hope the person in front of you is looking in his mirror.

So the nice policeman did the only thing he could do. He went through the red light. I am sure he had a special reason to do it, because why else would he have done it unless he was very, very special. But he did not have on his emergency lights so in theory he is supposed to ... you know, stop at the light, like the rest of us who are not special.

But he did have one thing that would have been turning red for sure as he looked in his mirror. His face.

The Great Actors

Wham. A shot blasts by your ear. That was close. You were almost hit.

You are watching a 3-D action adventure spy drama in a dark movie theatre.

This is real action, real life. This is what you happily pay to see.

Me too.

There are few things better than spending two hours watching some hero taking on the villains against impossible odds and then, at the last scary moment, saving the country and getting the girl. Or, if it is a modern movie, the girl uses her kung fu to save the entire earth, and then leaves the boy hungering as she walks away.

The only things better are the real stories.

I was passing by a movie wrapping, watching the extras leaving, when the star syndrome struck me. I knew one of them. I knew an actual extra in a Hollywood movie being shot in Vancouver.

He is Randy Tait, whom I wrote about before when he overcame a severe, almost deadly, drug habit and went on to help others who were in the same trouble he had escaped from.

Hello, hello, the usual.

"I didn't know you are an actor."

"It's Hollywood," he said, "without leaving home."

He said that after he quit heroin and cocaine and other chemicals life became so good he wanted all of it, and near the top was being in movies.

The only thing he wanted more was to help others. So he took some courses in drug counselling and became a Native counsellor and went to work helping. That is a good occupation.

"That is real life," he said. "But acting is being something you are not and trying to make it look like real life."

He went to an acting school and now stands with other extras through the rain and the night waiting for a moment to stand around on a sidewalk pretending to be a face in the crowd or in a back alley pretending he is a drug addict.

"I know how to do that," he said.

"Sometimes it's boring, but I'm in the movies. There was a time, you know, the only pictures I was in were mug shots. This is exciting," he said.

If Randy says something is exciting after the life he has had then it is exciting. I don't argue with Randy. He is bigger than me.

But talking with him reminded me of my favourite actor, another extra named Geoff Hopkins. He was sixteen years old during World War II. He lied about his age and sailed with the British Merchant Navy. The conditions were miserable aboard the ships and worse below in the oceans. That is where the submarines hunted for the underbellies of ships like those Geoff sailed on.

Jump ahead many years. He survived the war, he made a career selling insurance, he retired. And then the movie bug bit.

He got a job as an extra. In his first role he was supposed to cross a street after the car carrying the star passed by. His part was just a flicker of a second. He was a cog in the forward motion of the moving picture.

The director yelled "Action," the car went by, but Geoff did not cross the street.

"Cut!" The director was furious. A two-bit extra had ruined a scene.

"What the hell are you doing? You were supposed to cross the street."

Geoff looked at him standing more than a dozen steps away and then said, "The light said 'Don't Walk.'"

"I don't give a rat's ass what the light said, you cross when I tell you to cross," said the director.

He started the action again, but Geoff again refused to cross.

"The light was still red," he said.

The director was stammering, cursing, bursting. His words were hurting some ears. He threatened Geoff.

"You will never get work in this industry again," said the director.

Now you must put this real life picture in your mind: Geoff, who had looked over the waters of the Atlantic in wartime, who had stood on the bridge of a creaking supply ship at night searching the black ocean looking for a thin line of foam that would mean they would die if the captain did not rip the thin-hulled ship onto a different course, was facing an angry movie director.

He was not intimidated.

"I have to obey the law," he said.

The director pondered this for the smallest part of a second and said, "All right. Let's do it again, and see if the car can be timed to the light." He would not admit Geoff was right.

Geoff crossed with the light. He not only made the scene look legitimate; he kept the entire film industry honest, at least for a flicker of a second. He deserved an Oscar for crossing the street in the way it should be crossed.

I have forgotten what movie that was, but the scene of the street crossing is a triumph of bravery.

The sad note is that Geoff now has advanced Alzheimer's disease. He does not remember crossing the Atlantic or crossing the street. His wife spends her days with him. It is so hard to be with someone like that. The body is there, but the mind is not. Sort of like a newborn. Except with a newborn you see the future and hug the child who is starting to learn who you are. With an Alzheimer's sufferer you see the past and put your hand on a shoulder that has forgotten who you are.

Randy Tait standing in front of me, the hero in a real life drug war, and Geoff Hopkins living in my mind, the sailor who crossed the street, are the stories the movie industry only tries to portray. But it does not come close.

Lottery

won. I won the 6/49.

Just like in that commercial with the couple riding carefree on a new motorcycle.

"Honey, come here, we *won*," comes the voice-over while they ride on a bending road.

"We won what?"

"We won the Lotto 6/49."

Just like that. I had stuck the first of three tickets in the machine with the little red line that tells you if you've won, and I won.

I won $1.

I stuck in the second ticket. One dollar a second time. I had won twice. Impossible, but true.

This can't be. I have never had such luck. I have one ticket left. I haven't checked them for three weeks. The old fellows and gals are sitting on the bench looking up at the Keno numbers, which are a complete mystery to me.

I stick in the third. I know I am going to win big. *Big!* I once met a man who won the top prize *twice*—several million dollars followed by several million more dollars.

I met him while he was buying more tickets. He was in a corner grocery store. He paid $50 or $60 for this round. I had heard he would put down the same amount at another store later in the day. I thought I could never spend that much, even for a million dollars.

Then I heard he had a son living in a basement apartment in another province. His son was hooked on crack cocaine. His father was sending him money to keep him alive. Poor father. Poor son.

The father did not win that time, or ever again, at least not big-time winning. I thought about money buying happiness and stopped thinking.

But now I had one more ticket and I knew that a streak could not be broken. I have met many gamblers at the track. They are my favourite betters. They look at something living and take a chance on it. They are not folks who put money in a machine and let electronics decide their future. Horse betters know about lung power and the ability of a jockey to hold onto a pair of leather straps while an animal is running at 60 kilometres an hour beneath him and if he falls off he will be killed. *That* is a gamble.

If you fall off your chair in front of a slot machine they just pick you up and you continue betting. No challenge.

I checked my third ticket. One dollar. I had won again.

It was the luckiest I have ever been. Three dollars on three tickets that only cost me $12 in Mini Dips.

There is no point to this story except that you have been there. After thirty years of the lottery being in BC I have won $2 numerous times and $1 three times in a row.

Okay, there *is* a point to this story. That is it.

The Secret Tree

Okay, it won't be a secret any more. It was not a secret after we put it on television. But, really, it was too late to kill it.

At the Kitsilano tennis courts, I was told, there was a wonderful man I had to meet. He played every day but, more important, he also changed the world.

He is a little bit crazy. He sneaks up behind other players and barks. They jump, then they realize it is Alex and they laugh.

If someone is in a heavy-duty game he doesn't do that—there are limits on being a clown—but if you are just warming up, watch out.

"I like to make them laugh," he said.

But he does something else. In the spring he carries seeds—flower seeds—and wherever he goes he spreads the seeds. Very often they are a wide range of flowers, and usually the longest-lasting ones he can buy.

When he goes through a back alley or a little strip of dirt near a building he sprinkles some seeds. He tries to cover them with a little dirt that he scratches up, sometimes just with his shoe, but sometimes he just lets them rest on the ground, as nature gets away with.

Later in the summer, wherever he walks, there are flowers. Very nice.

He also breaks the Park Board's rules. He plants his seeds in the little strip of dirt around the edge of the tennis courts.

"Shush," he said. "Don't tell."

But we have to tell. This old man who plays tennis is the reason the edge of the tennis courts is so pretty.

A while ago I met two sweet ladies who decorated a tree in Stanley Park every Christmas. They put balls and ribbons on the branches and made it look beautiful. It was at the edge of the parking lot at Third Beach.

They also put socks and mittens in plastic bags and tied them to the tree.

"For the homeless," they said.

The Park Board took down the decorations.

The ladies put them back.

Board took them down again.

Ladies put them up again.

The administration in charge of keeping the parks in shape for all people did the only thing it could. It sent in gardeners with a chainsaw and cut down the tree.

"Don't you dare try to put Christmas on a tree."

I don't know if they said that, but with the stump being the only thing left, that was generally the idea.

I bring this up because Alex, the fellow at the tennis court, did not only plant flowers.

Right outside the fence, on the beach side of the court, is a beautiful birch tree, higher than the top of the fence around the tennis players.

"I put that there," he said.

"What?" I said, knowing what happens when you are kind to a tree in a city park.

"Ten years ago," he said.

"And they didn't chop it down?"

"They never noticed," he said.

I was worried that after it was on television the Board officials might sneak in at night and whisper, "Timber," as they cut it down by the glow of flashlights. But it survived.

Maybe they were aware of the legend of the dog with the growl and the loud bark that always hangs around those tennis courts and that tree and seems to protect them. No one has ever seen the dog, but if you ever heard it bark you'd know it is big.

Doggie Bags

This is a totally disgusting story and I advise you not to read it. Or at least not if you are under six years old.

It happened in David Lam Park, which is the breathing space for many of the new condos in Yaletown. This is the only patch of grass left along that whole side of False Creek. And since it is the only patch available, everyone who has a dog goes there to walk their dog.

Dogs are now very fashionable to have in small apartments. Dog owners meet in the park right after work. Big dogs and little dogs, all out for the first time since morning, run and jump and fetch balls and have a wonderful time. Dogs are neat.

They also do what all dogs do when they get outside. On the grass they do what they have not been doing all day. And the people who take their dogs there are all, each and everyone, conscientious. They all bring little plastic baggies to pick up what their dogs do.

Now, let's say that again. They pick up what *their* dogs do, not what other dogs do, and here is the problem.

A man and a woman, each carrying plastic baggies, each standing on opposite sides of a pile that was on the grass were discussing said pile.

"That's not mine," said the woman.

"Well, it's not mine," said the man.

"My Goldie always goes over there," said the woman.

"My dog's do doesn't look like that," said the man. "I know what my dog does and that's not it."

"If you just pick it up we can get on with our evening," said the woman.

Now I was not there at the beginning, so I do not know how this standoff started. I do not know if one dog was squatting while the other dog owner was watching or if both dog owners just happened to look up at the same time and then look down and presto, they both discovered something at the same time. I don't know.

I only know that as I walked across the park I heard the above, and what continues.

"I will not pick it up," said the man. "I know that is not mine."

You can begin to see where territorial disputes lead to wars.

The man said he feeds his dog, whose name is George, with food from specialty pet shops. "That," he said referring to the do on the ground, "comes from dried dog food."

"Well I mix my Goldie's food myself and I know that did not come from her and I am not picking it up."

"Well, it's not mine either," said the man. "I know what George does."

All around them dog owners were walking with their baggies. These are not only socially conscious people, but they are ecologically trendy. They must not only pick up what their dogs do, but they must be seen carrying a full bag of do. It is sort of a sign of civic accomplishment. If you leave a park with a bag with nothing in it you look like an environmental leper. And walking away from something at your feet is abandoning a civic obligation—a basic social crime.

"What are we going to do about this?" asked the woman pointing to the unclaimed pile. "It is definitely not mine."

And then from the group of dog owners stepped a woman with a mutt. She had been listening.

"I'll get it," she said. She did not say, "Grow up you two." She did not shake her head in disgust. She had a gentle tone that was so powerful in its lack of accusation that both the man and the woman must have felt ridiculous.

Then the woman with the extra bag walked away with her mutt waving his tail. There are some wonderful people still in the world.

And then the park cleared out. The allotted time for walking was over and dinner from the microwave was waiting. Everyone left except the man and the woman.

They each had empty bags. During the dispute neither dog had apparently done what they came to do, or they had somehow done it without being seen doing it, and neither owner could leave until their bag had something in it.

An empty baggie would be a sign of guilt. It might mean your dog had somehow gone without you watching, and we must watch our dogs do the one thing we would never watch ourselves do even if we could, which we can't.

Worse, an empty bag might be seen by someone who would know that you were leaving without taking away what you should not leave behind. And you would have to come back to the park the next day, and you know what folks would say.

As I left I saw them both walking around the park, urging George and Goldie to do something. Please.

It is wonderful to have a dog, but it is not easy to explain human behaviour to them. How do you get them to understand the humiliation of going home without the one thing that your dog went out to leave behind?

George Hollinger

Chris Gailus said, "Ouch. How did he get his leg up so high?"

Squire said, "That hurt."

Deb clapped.

Wayne smiled and shook his head in admiration.

Those are the judges. The Supreme Court of TV. If they like it, it is good.

George just skated away and got ready for the next slapshot.

George Hollinger. We will not fool around and keep his age a secret until the end. George is eighty-two. George not only skates three times a week, he plays hockey. He elbows, gently. He blocks, aggressively. He shoots, fanatically.

"When did you learn to skate?" I asked, assuming that he grew up on skates.

"When I was forty. My son taught me," he said.

I did not know the next question. This happens when the story suddenly becomes bigger than my preconceived thoughts on how the story should go.

I think in the humble ordinary terms that most of us talk in.

It is imperative to humbly say, "I learned to skate before I could walk."

If you are really going for the Aw, shucks factor, "I learned to skate (or ride a horse) before I could crawl."

If they really want to impress you with their incredible natural talent, "I was born knowing how to wrestle alligators."

And for the very few who live in a world of super impressions, "I was an incredible ten-pin bowler while I was still inside my mother's womb. She bowled and I listened to the strikes in my amniotic fluid."

But poor George, thirty-nine and never been skating. At forty he watched his son and thought he would try it. At fifty he joined an old-timers' hockey league. At sixty he was the oldest member. At seventy, well into retirement, he started playing three times a week. At eighty he never missed a Monday, Wednesday or Friday game.

At eighty-two, while he was standing on the ice and I was behind the wooden wall in the players' box, I asked him how long he will keep playing.

"I hope to make it to eighty-three," he said.

Then he lifted one of his legs up to the top of the wall and leaned forward to stretch the muscles at the back of his leg.

That was when Chris Gailus said "Ouch."

The moral of the story? You don't really need to ask. You know what it is. It doesn't matter when you start, start anything. The only thing that matters is that you don't stop.

To Laugh, and To Be Sad

I have a rule. It was on the cover of a recent book, so you know it is for real, and really important to me.

"Any kid who steps in front of the camera gets on television."

That is pretty clear and simple.

I don't want a child thinking she is going to be on television, which is a very big thing in a child's life, and then watching the story only to find she is not there. The same with a boy child. They are sensitive and trusting.

On Sunday, May 21, 2012, the Cloverdale Rodeo was on. I love the rodeo. Some don't. I do, but I have done many rodeo stories about cowboys and cowgirls and horses and hats and hoofs. What is different?

We walked onto the fairway and heard a large fellow laughing. He was eating a hot dog and he guffed and howled and belted out a delicious sound of happiness.

There is no way in writing to describe a laugh. It just is. It comes from the heart and mind and ribs and bursts out and makes you and everyone around you feel good. That is not bad for a universal human emotion.

After capturing his laugh I heard the woman who sold him his hot dog laughing.

"I always laugh. It makes me feel good," she said.

Her name was Joyce, and her laugh made me feel good.

Then we turned around and saw a girl about twelve laughing. She was laughing at the hot dog woman laughing.

"Do you really feel that good?" I asked.

She nodded and laughed again.

I hate to say that never have I heard such happiness, but never have I heard such happiness. She was a delight. She was happy. She made the story.

Thank you.

We walked away looking for something that would make the story look like a rodeo as well as a carnival with a hot dog stand.

Nearby, the women who ride in the opening parade were circling in a paddock. We got pictures of that. Then I saw a lone cowboy walking up the path. He had a worn-out cowboy hat and dusty boots and was lean and leathery. You don't get more cowboy than that.

"How does a cowboy laugh?" I asked.

"I don't know. I'm not a cowboy."

"Well, who are you?"

"I'm with them," he said, pointing to the paddock.

"With the horses?"

"No, with the women."

For a brief, very brief, moment I thought, "There's nothing wrong with that."

He didn't look like a fill-in for the all-women riding team, but who am I to judge?

"I'm a boyfriend of one of the girls."

"Oh," I said, and he probably figured out what I was thinking by the involuntarily relieved laugh that came from me.

The editor heard that in the dark edit room and laughed.

That is great, I thought. If he laughs then everyone will, because editors listen to the worst and the best of stuff all day and hardly blink.

I asked the cowboy to get his girlfriend to laugh. She tried but could not do it on cue. She called another woman rider who also could not laugh. This was very funny. Then they called another who did laugh. That was even funnier.

Thank you, thank you.

"And at the end of the story will go this precious little girl who has the best laugh of all and I will say, 'But the best laugh was from one little girl who sounded like she loved laughing.'"

"Where is that?" asked the editor.

"Somewhere near the beginning. Somewhere after the man with the hot dog and the pictures of the fairway."

He rewound the pictures. It is no longer tape. It does not actually rewind. The images are in a computer cloud and are brought to the edit room by magical means.

"Where?" he asked.

I looked. There were pictures of the man with the hot dog and pictures of the fairway, but no pictures of the little girl with the giant bust of happiness.

"It has to be there," I said.

He looked again.

"It must be."

He went through the pictures slowly, slower than recorded speed. We saw the man with the hot dog in slow motion and then the fairway in slow motion. It was painful. My heart was sinking.

The new, ultra-technological cameras have no moving parts. When a picture is being recorded there is a tiny red spot in the upper right-hand corner of the small viewfinder in the camera. But when a news cameraman, or woman, is shooting there is a great deal going on. There is the scene and the focus and the colour balance and the monitoring of the sound and the holding of the camera steady on a shoulder that has carried twenty-five pounds of metal for most of its adult life and there is the tenseness to protect yourself if someone hits you from the side or behind. There is all that, and sometimes you miss something, like the little red spot.

Especially you might miss it because the new cameras do not have tape that is turning while the record button is on. The new cameras have no moving parts. The only way to know if it is recording is that tiny red spot.

The camera was not on. The record button had been hit once and then, in a computer-indoctrinated way, the button was hit almost instantly a second time. It was turned off.

The little girl who made the story, who went home to watch herself in the story, was not in the story.

I sat in the room asking the story god to make it unhappen. Please, put her somewhere else in the dots and dashes of the cloud and make her appear.

It did not work.

I said in the last line of the story, which was over the horses riding away, that there were many other super laughs that we could not get on TV. I hoped that helped the girl with the happy face. I know she was disappointed. I know she can live through that disappointment. There will be bigger disappointments in life. But this one was not her fault.

I also know that I hope that little girl reads this line now so I can tell her, she was the best. And I apologize.

What do we all learn from this? Sometimes real big hurts were never meant to be.

Mystery Twitter Story

The world has been taken over by Twitter. So will be books. Done in 140 words, counting quotes and periods.

Dark and stormy.
And then.
Shots rang out.
And then.
Screams.
And then.
Screeching tires.
And then.
"Don't move."
And then.
"Guilty."
And then.

Escape.
And then.
Dark and Stormy 2 in 3D.
No kidding. Just you wait.

And if you like that one, how about:

Comedy Twitter

Two men.
One woman.
One baby.
Family Reunion.
Two Mothers In-Law.
Law suit.
Religious beliefs.
No blood. No DNA.
Mother leaves.
(It's a comedy)
Fathers become
Mothers.
Kid grows.
Parent-Teacher conferences.
"Are you gay? We need gay parents."
Gays are In.
"Not gay," they say.
"Please *say* you are gay."
Fathers say, "Just friends."
"Too late. Twitter sent."
Kids rally.
Parents protest.
Fathers protest.

Gay groups protest.
Girl grows.
Wedding.
Fathers cry.
Mother returns.
With real father
Of the bride.
Men go fishing, together.

Twitter will take over the world.

Okay, whoops. You saw the mistake. I did not know until I told a friend about this and he asked if I had Twitter and I said no and he said, "No, idiot. 140 *characters* maximum, not 140 *words*."

So:

Dark and stormy.
Guns.
Screams.
Screeching.
Caught.
Guilty.
Escape.
To be continued.

And comedy:
Two men,
One baby.
Mom leaves.
Men gay?
Support.
Protest.
Girl grows.
Wedding.

Tears.
Real Poppa.
2 Fathers
Fishing,
Together.
(The sequel)
Third enters
With fishing rod.

Actually, it gets better with brevity.

Oscar, Please Don't Wash, Ever

Old boxes of stuff from kids should be taken with them when they go.

"Come on, do you think we have a junkyard here? Take your stuff and get rid of it."

But one was left behind, so I peeked.

Some baseball cards, some batteries that luckily did not leak. Leaky batteries can ruin a good box of stuff. If you don't know what a leaky battery is, you are young.

In the old days if you left a battery laying around long enough the goo from the inside would often ooze to the outside and you would be very disappointed that the photographs that the battery was left lying on would never be seen again.

In fact you could never touch them again.

There, now you know. New batteries don't leak, which is a major advance in science.

There were some popsicle sticks that could be made into a raft and floated down a creek if you had a creek. And there were some matches hidden under an envelope. The envelope had some scribbling on it. You know if you scribble on an envelope no one will ever look underneath it. That is a well-known fact when you are young, so you can hide your matches under there.

If you have matches you can do anything, but most of all you have to hide them because you know, "If that kid gets hold of a book of matches he could burn down the house."

That is a very powerful thing to have in your secret box of stuff, even though you would never burn down the house. In fact, the only time you tried to light a match it was raining and you couldn't even keep the match going, much less a house.

Growing up is secret. And it has secret boxes and secret places and you were watching *Sesame Street*, which was the only program your parents wanted you to watch. Despite that it was still good.

Bert and Ernie were there every day and they taught you things. They had nice voices. And there was Oscar the Grouch. He had a rough voice. It was scary at first, but then you got to like Oscar more than all the other characters because he did what you really wished you could do.

He lived in a garbage can, and inside that can he had everything. He had old shoes and old carrots and old books and everything. He had a swimming pool in there and a bowling alley.

He lived in his secret place.

And then time passed. *Sesame Street* is not the same.

I meet Bob McGrath every year at the Variety Telethon, and of all the important people there he is the most important. My kids grew up with him. He taught them patience and laughter and things a parent is sometimes too busy and worried to do.

He told me he could never start another *Sesame Street*, not like in the old days. There were only three or four kids' shows back in the

1960s. Now there are, Bob thought for a moment, "So many even Oscar could not count them."

There was something else he did not say. The forces that want to change the world to the way they see it went to work on *Sesame Street*.

Bert and Ernie were gay and hiding in the closet. Split them up.

The answer from the show: No.

Oscar was depressed and gave a negative image living in the dirt of a can. Take him out and clean him up.

Answer: No.

It is good that some stand up for closets and trash cans.

And then, in a corner of the box of stuff left behind, there was sock with a hole in it. Something was inside.

Out came a plastic toy of Oscar. His head and shoulders were just above the top of the can. In his left hand was a paper airplane.

Inside the secret world of an old sock, which was inside a box of secret stuff, was the fellow with his secret world inside a trash can, in which there was everything.

I was very lucky that box was left behind.

The box is now returned to its dark corner on the floor of the closet where I found it. I left the matches. I think the house will be okay. But there is one thing missing, of course.

Oscar is on my desk, just a small move away from my right hand. And as soon as he feels like it, as soon as he stops being so grouchy, he may tell me about more things he has down there in his can. I cannot see them. He can.

So can you.

Funny How Things Work Out

I was visiting my friends across the street after they came back from a trip to Germany. They have relatives there. They brought me back a beer stein with "1, 2, g'suffa!" written on the front.

"What's it mean?" they asked.

"Eins, zwei, DRINK," I said.

It is the most famous of all beer hall songs in German history. Drinking beer is a way of life in Germany, just as drinking wine is in France and Italy.

It is not binge drinking or drunkenness or swilling back shots. Beer in Germany and wine in France and Italy are a way of life. In Germany you drink beer on your lunch hour in the company cafeteria.

You buy bottles of wine at a highway gas station in France. You buy them from a rack by the gas pumps where you don't have to get out of your car. You reach out the window and grab a bottle.

I started drinking beer in Germany. The first one I had I poured down the sink. Ugh. I was fourteen. I had tasted whiskey before (don't go there), but not beer. However, it wasn't long before beer became a daily drink with my mother at dinner. Hard to believe.

Beer halls were also a way of life in Germany, but I never went into one when I lived there. It was not that I was too young, it was just that all the folks in there were too old, or were tourists who were starting to go back to Germany.

But this story is not about drinking. It is about something else that Germans do. They make bread. If you go into a German bakery you will see twenty or more, probably many more, different types of bread. Each is wonderful. Each looks like a piece of art. Each looks like you could live on it forever.

And there may also be three or four dessert cakes and cookies. Germans are not big on desserts.

If you go to France, on the other hand, there are twenty or more kinds of dessert cakes and cookies. Each is wonderful. Each looks like a piece of art. Each looks like you could live on it forever.

And in there will be one bread—the baguette.

It is what makes multiculturalism impossible, but wonderful.

I lived in Munich a decade after the war. You know that. You have read the stories. Bombed-out buildings were everywhere. You do not have to read an anti-war novel to know war is not good for babies or buildings or anything. It took the Germans ten years to clear the rubble out of the streets, and the only place they could throw the broken bricks was back onto the sidewalks.

The street I lived on had one surviving apartment house. It had bullet holes across the front. Every other building for block after block was gone, or only the outside shell was left. I walked up and down my street looking up through the buildings and seeing the sky. It was eerie.

But across from the apartment house was a bakery. It was the only tiny building left on that side of the street. Every day I bought bread, and it was the best I ever had. I have lived more than half a century since then and there is still nothing that comes close to their bread.

I told my wife and kids about this bakery the whole time we all lived together, which was a long time, until the kids moved out.

"You are not going to tell us about the bakery again, are you?"

That was a frequent line, but I did not care. The things I like, I talk about.

The bakery was my grounding spot. I made friends with some of the people who worked there. I learned some of the language. But most of all, I had this great fresh bread that did not need anything else. If you added a sausage or a pickle it was a meal.

Many years later I got a chance to go back to Munich with my wife and daughter. We could only be there for a day, so the heck with all the sights and important places, I would take them to the bakery. Also, they could see the apartment where I lived, but that would be boring compared to the place of bread.

I rented a car, and we got there quickly.

"That's where I lived. Wow. It is a beautiful building now with buildings next to it. There were only holes there when I left. And look at all the gardens and a bicycle path. But forget about all that. Let's cross the street. That's the bakery over there. Wait until you taste their bread."

But something was wrong.

It was dark.

We crossed and slowly approached a storefront that had been my oasis in a foreign land. There was no aroma of bread. The windows were empty.

Closed. It was Sunday, and Germany still has that quaint old Canadian tradition. The shops, big and small, take off one day a week. What???!!! How could they?

We drove back to the centre of town and went to the Hofbräuhaus, the most famous beer hall in the country. Inside we joined the Japanese tourists and, for the first time in my life, I sang, "1, 2, g'suffa!"

In Germany beer is considered to be liquid bread.

It did not come close to the bakery.

The Secret Garden

There is a time to kill, they say, and a time to heal. A time for war and a time for peace.

I don't know what that means. The first time I heard it I thought it was okay to kill and have wars because there was an approved time for them. And if it says in the Bible that there is a time for them then they must be okay, even though I know they are not.

But then I met Brian and saw what he had done and I could only think there was a time for that.

On the morning of September 11, 2001, Brian watched the airplane crash into the tower. The other tower was already burning. He watched and he hurt and he tried not to watch but could not turn away from the television.

That is what most of us did.

Brian Whitehouse was an alcoholic. Brian was a roofer. Alcoholics are not praised in our world. In fact, they are not the stars anywhere.

And roofers are generally joked about as needing only one qualification for the job: absolutely no fear of death. I got that from an ex-roofer who became a gardener. He said some roofs are steeper than the mountains some climbers get their pictures taken on.

But then came the airplanes and the buildings falling and the pain and all that—I don't have to elaborate. Almost all of us watched it on television. We were not there. Brian did not suffer any more than the rest of us.

But then he went outside into the back lane behind his home. It was not really a back lane. It was, and still is, an easement about thirty feet wide and a block long that was just there. It was fenced-off city property that was left over on some municipal map. It did not belong to the homeowners and the city had no use for it. No one walked there, not even dog owners. It was filled with blackberries and garbage.

Brian pulled out some of the brambles. He cut his hand. He got gloves and garden shears and fought his way into the thorns. Thoughts of dying and sirens and disbelief were in the scrapes and scratches on his arms. Nothing made sense.

He kept it up until he was exhausted.

Many people did something similar after seeing others throw themselves out of windows high in the sky and watching two giant towers crash back to earth while thousands were still inside. Many had to do something, anything. Some punched walls. Some drank. Some prayed. Some cried. Some stared at the sky. Some told little children who were watching not to watch. Brian pulled out blackberries.

The next day he pulled out more, and the next and the next. He shovelled away garbage and cleaned up rotting, stinking messes.

Ten years later I heard about the Secret Garden of Boundary Bay. I had seen other secret gardens. They are all nice, some incredibly so. Most of them were only open on invitation. Brian did not block entrance to anyone. In fact, he couldn't. He did not own the land. He had no more right to be there than anyone else.

But when I saw his garden it was more than any description can contain. Beautiful, yes. Incredible, yes, but so much more. Go on the internet. There are some pictures, but none of them conveys the feeling of peace and beauty that you have when you walk into the back lane that was once filled with thorns and garbage.

In another book I wrote about a fellow named Jason who did the same thing under the Burrard Street Bridge. He cleared out the homeless encampments and the bottles and the filthy debris and planted a garden where there was no soil, no sun and no rain.

There is nothing like a challenge. For soil he got used coffee grounds from Starbucks and mixed them with peat moss that he bought himself. For rain he attached a hose, with permission, to an outside spigot of the Aquatic Centre. And for sun he got plants that did well with little of it.

Like Brian, Jason drank too much, way too much. And he was overweight, grossly overweight. By the time I met him he no longer drank and was as slim as a model or an athlete, or a guy who turned a sidewalk slum into a place of beauty.

When I met Brian he had a similar story. He was drinking water. No more alcohol. If you drink, just try that. It is an unbelievable fight with yourself.

I wrote about the struggle that Constance Barnes had doing that earlier in this book. Brian, like Constance, was an alcoholic and now he does not drink. Now he has his garden.

"If he is not home he is in his garden," said his wife, who remembers when he wasn't.

And he is now a retired roofer. What does a roofer know about gardening? Nothing. What does he know about plants? Nothing. Landscaping? The same.

But his garden is a work of genius. I got that review from some landscaping friends of mine who are also geniuses in their art.

And now wedding photos are taken in the garden, and neighbours walk their dogs there and some have picnics.

I asked two women, who were spreading a cloth on the grass to have lunch, if they knew anything about this garden.

"No, it is probably a city park, but a very nice park," one said.

I wrote the story for television. I could think of only one way to tell it.

"There is a time for war, some say, and a time for peace. A time to tear down and a time to build up."

I am still not sure what that means, but I know that after the war there is a time for peace and a time for healing. This I do know, Brian is spending the rest of his life in that time.

The Secret Garden is at 67A Street and Fourth Avenue, in Boundary Bay. There are no locks on the door.

Reilly's Method Works

She wrote a nice letter saying I go to bed with her mother every night. I did not show it to my wife.

She said her mother liked my stories and had my books and would I autograph them.

Of course. If we are going to bed together I should certainly share my penmanship. It is not very warm or cuddly, but a little ink should be shared by bedmates. But they live in Mission and I work in Burnaby and I don't have much free time to drive to Mission.

She is taking her mother to the orchid show at VanDusen Garden. That is perfect. I will do a story on the orchid show and sign her books.

This is an aside and it is not part of this story, but have you ever looked at an orchid? I mean looked really close, and studied it and thought, "Oh my gosh. That looks like a part of a woman's anatomy!"

You do not need to stretch the imagination to see it, and it is beautiful, and mesmerizing. Not all orchids are like that, but most are.

Not all certain parts of a woman's anatomy are like an orchid either, but most are.

This revelation came to me while I was doing a story on an orchid show, almost thirty years ago, and it was the first time I had ever seen orchids, much less been to a show. As always I was looking at the people who were at the show, because it is the people who make the stories, and then I glanced at one of the flowers.

"Can't be," I thought.

I glanced at another.

"Oh, come on. I am not seeing what I think I am seeing. This can't be. It really can't."

There were mostly sweet little old ladies at the show and what I was seeing—what they were looking at—were pictures from old *Penthouse* centrefolds, back in the day when *Penthouse* had a centrefold and what you saw there was something you did not see anywhere else.

And now I saw it again, growing out of a pot.

The thought, isn't nature wonderful, came to mind, but I really did not want anything else clouding my mind. I just wanted to look at the orchids.

I am not allowed to say the thoughts that went through me as I looked at orchids for the first time, but I am allowed to say I understand honeybees, and I am jealous.

Sadly, the Sunday of the orchid show at which I was to meet the woman who had written to me about her mother was also the Sunday of the Sun Run and I have not missed doing something about that for the past twenty years. What's more, I had my granddaughter Ruby sleeping at our home and I had asked if she wanted to come to work with me and she had said yes. The race would be the most fun for her and I completely forgot about signing the books for the nice lady who lives in Mission.

Darn. When I remembered I said, "Darn."

I called. She forgave me. She was nice. We made arrangements for a few Sundays later to meet in Port Moody, halfway for each of us.

But then came the Vancouver Marathon, and I always do a story on that.

"Sorry."

She forgave me, again. Then I suggested that the following Sunday, no matter what I did a story about, she and her mother could come to the television station and take a tour and I would sign her books.

We met in the parking lot a week later.

"See," said the nice daughter. "The Reilly method works."

"What do you mean?"

I know I wrote about getting what you want if you believe you will get it, just as the snot-nosed kid taught me, but I had postponed this poor woman twice.

"I got what I wanted," she said. "Reilly also said you have to be patient."

Kid Behind the Wheel

This was so good. You had to see it. There is no story, just something to see.

I drove into the parking lot of the PNE in March and the winds were blowing and the bare branches in the trees were being forced back and forth so far I swore they would break.

Then, crack, one broke. It was nasty out. The litter in the parking lot looked like whatever tumbleweeds would have looked like on the open prairies of the old west in a storm.

There was a row of trucks, which was not unusual here. This is a staging area for long-haul transport and short-haul stopping off to figure out what packages go where. It is a working lot.

Then I looked in the windshield of one of the worn-out campers and saw a picture that would get on the cover of *National Geographic* if they were doing a feature on the parking lots of North America.

A little girl, maybe two years old, was standing on the front seat holding onto the steering wheel and pulling it left and right. But what was magical was the smile of pure joy on her face. Out of a row of trucks and windshields, that smile was the only thing you could see. She was pulling the wheel and laughing and her hair was flopping back and forth. I was way over here in my car and she was way over there and all the windows were rolled up but she was laughing. I didn't have to hear it to know it.

I kept driving by, thinking of *National Geographic* because their most famous cover of all time was a young Afghan girl, a refugee in Pakistan, with a scarf over the top of her head and with a stare—into the camera, into the universe—that will never fade. You have probably seen the picture. If not, look up *National Geographic* on your computer and put in "famous cover photos." You will see it and say, "Oh, yes, of course. That is beautiful."

The little girl behind the steering wheel would come in a close second. The famous magazine cover had sadness, poverty and total hypnotic entrapment.

The girl in the windshield had only joy, the total rapture of being a little girl. But you could add to that poverty, because it was a worn-out camper that she was in and it was in a line of carnival trucks that exist in a world of bare existence.

I drove by and saw her for less than three seconds. A few minutes later I met a cameraman who was waiting in another parking lot at the fair and told him he had to see this picture. It was beautiful. It was amazing. It was art.

I knew it would probably be gone by the time we got back because things like that don't last. Nothing is as good the second time. Nothing is the same when you tell someone about it and then try to get them to see what you have seen.

This happens every time, and I mean every time, that someone tells me something wonderful.

"The cat jumped out of the tree and landed in my arms. I didn't even see it coming."

But when I get the lady who caught the cat together with someone with a camera, things change.

"What did you just tell me?"

"Well, I was walking down the street, as I usually do. Did you know this street is a little uneven and you could trip on it?"

"What about the cat?"

"Oh, yes, I was walking down the street and there was a cat in the tree. Now, mind you, I don't like cats."

"But, please, what happened."

"As I was saying, I was walking on the street and went under this tree, or was it that tree? Anyway, suddenly..."

This is the moment. I knew it would come. I know the camera is on. We will capture the moment that is coming now.

"Suddenly... by the way, do you want me to tell you how the cat came out of the tree or how I caught it?"

That happens every time. You cannot restage reality. When someone tells you something that is exciting, that is your lucky moment. Your only job is to pay attention, stop talking and listen, and then you will remember it and enjoy it. Don't do stupid things like reporters do who try to get people to recreate the excitement of telling you that whatever it is.

I feared the same was going to happen with the little girl behind the wheel. The chances of her being there five minutes after I had seen her were non-existent.

We drove back. She was there. She was still steering and laughing and life was worth living.

The cameraman got out and started taking her picture while I searched out a parent to make sure we could do what we were doing.

The father, I assumed, was near the cab of the old camper. He had a baseball cap on his head and a cigarette in his mouth. He was a carnie.

"I've come from Nova Scotia and we were hoping for good weather," he said.

Carnies travel. They are the gypsies of our society. They pull trailers that turn into rides or side-show games of balloon popping and then they pack up and travel to the next city. They do this for most of their lives. Along the way they have babies.

"That little girl is yours?"

"There are five of them in the cab," he said.

I had not seen any of the others. One was four months old, the others were too big to play with the steering wheel and were sitting back in the front seat waiting, just waiting, as they have done much of their lives.

They wait to get to another town. They wait for their parents to start working and then to stop working. And sometimes they wait for the weather to clear up.

Unless you are two. Then you don't wait. You hold the steering wheel and pull it back and forth and laugh.

How much story is there in one face? Basically, the universal story. Children survive, luckily for us, because that is why we are here. We were children, once.

There was nothing else in the story on television that night. Just pictures of the little girl and my conversation with her father. Her mother was also in the front seat, but covered by children, and she did not want to be interviewed.

How much story is there in that? I don't have to elaborate. You know. Too many children in too little space and time.

And yet, one of her children was giggling and steering and laughing and staring out with eyes that were hypnotic. Three years later I still remember how she looked.

If you find that cover of *National Geographic*, just replace the face with that of a happy two-year-old. Same eyes, except the ones in the cab of the camper were smiling.

Secret Admirer

She is still doing it. And she will probably keep doing it until the twelfth of never, and that, you know, is a long, long time. She proves that you do not need a publisher or a newspaper or television station to get your words out there.

When I met her she said she hoped she would be able to keep it up for a few more years. That was twenty years ago.

Dorothy Walton is the saint of Valentine's Day. A long time ago she was the manager of a West End apartment building. She said she had seen many single elderly lonely people living there.

So a week before Valentine's Day she got some construction paper and cut out pictures of flowers from a few magazines. She pasted the flowers on the paper and wrote "From A Secret Admirer."

"I slipped them under a few doors and the next day there were so many smiles it was beautiful," she said.

So the next year she started earlier and collected more magazines, and a month before Valentine's Day she began cutting and pasting and she added some angels and cupids and hearts to the flowers.

And she wrote a poem:

"I will love you 'til farmers stop plowing,
'til dollars stop shrinking
And kittens stop meowing,
Until everyone's healthy
And no one gets sick
And the Queen stirs her tea
With a popsicle stick!
Happy Valentine's Day
From a secret admirer."

She slipped them under every door in the building.

The next day everyone was smiling.

She continued this for several years until she noticed that there were sad people in the next building.

You can guess what happened. She started a month earlier and gave a card to everyone there. And a few years later she moved to the next building. In time she was making a card for everyone on her street.

I talked to some of the beloved. They did not know who made the cards, but they were happy to get them.

"This is the only Valentine I get," said one little old lady. "It means the world to me."

Later, much later, Dorothy and her husband retired and moved to the Okanagan, and there he died. But she kept making cards. She doesn't make as many now because many of the recipients have passed on and because it is expensive to buy so many stamps, but there are a few who still get cards, and I am lucky enough to be one of them. This year it said:

"I will love you 'til Smarties are dumb,
Until all Stand Up comics fall on their bum,

'Til the Waldorf's Lunch menu is sardines on toast
And the dinner surprise is a marshmallow roast.
From your secret admirer."
So much goodness she gives and when I open my card I always say,
"I wonder who loves me so?"
And then I feel warm all over.
I have written about her before, but how can you pass up remembering a story like that?

The Fighter

"Amazing Grace" was being played on a guitar by a nun. It could not have been sweeter.

The song was being sung in an old Catholic church just off East Hastings Street. A casket on a dolly with wheels was rolled down the aisle. We don't carry caskets any more. Even the humble boxes of forever have grown heavier with more trim and metal, and we the living have grown weaker.

That would have been a joke to Doreen, who was inside the casket. She liked to poke fun at the oddities of life. She was a writer. She was not a published writer, but she was a writer of everything she saw. She had journals and stacks of paper and notes on simply everything.

"It is all so interesting," she told me one day over coffee at an old diner.

"What is so interesting?" I asked.

She looked at me as though I understood nothing.

"Everything," she said. "Just everything."

She was in the Trout Lake Writers Group and, even though she was in her eighties and could only get around on an electric scooter and had to breathe with the help of an oxygen tank, she would read her latest insights to the group and then listen to others with total attention.

She was the kind of member every club wishes for—active when it was her turn and quiet when it wasn't.

But the best thing about her, at least the best thing I knew, was that she was a plain old street fighter. Here's the story.

There was a handicap parking spot right under the window of her second-floor apartment. She did not like people without a handicapped sticker parking there. That is a very simple concept, and most of us feel the same way, but Doreen would park her scooter on the sidewalk next to the spot and confront those who parked there who did not have a handicapped sticker. Most of us would not do that. It could end up in an argument, and we don't want that.

What would happen if some big guy parked there and we said you shouldn't do that and he told us to mind our own flippin' business? And suppose at the same time he took a step toward us and he said what are you going to do about it?

Or suppose someone said they were just going to be a minute while they went to the bank and they really had to get there and they had never done this before and they hadn't noticed the sign and they walked away and ignored us?

Or suppose they said they had a sticker but had forgotten it and then they walked away with no cane or crutch. Are we going to say "You are not handicapped!" Are we going to take that chance and wind up with a defamation suit because their father-in-law is handicapped and they are going to pick him up and get his sticker and put it in the blankety blank windshield and you will be hearing from their lawyer?

So we do nothing.

Doreen did not care. She did something. Often she would just sit and wag her index finger back and forth, just a no-no to the driver. The silent message delivered with eloquence.

One day she was trying to get on a special bus for people with wheelchairs and scooters but the bus could not get close enough to the curb because someone was parked in that spot. Her scooter overturned and she fell out and her face hit the blacktop of the street and the tire of a truck turning the corner just missed her head.

"I saw the wheel and thought I would be crushed," she said.

Luck, timing, or the grace of something saved her.

After that she became a warrior, the defender of the spot. She was out every day. She got a petition going. She wrote about the parking spot in her journal. She told her writers club about it. And she kept wagging her finger.

And it worked. When you fight for something, fight hard and long and believe in what you are doing and are not afraid, the results are amazing. It doesn't matter whether you read examples of this in the Old Testament or see it in the *Rambo* movies or *Karate Kid* or in some alcoholic trying to get his life back; if you fight hard enough you usually win.

If you don't fight you usually lose.

Doreen's protected parking spot was increasingly free of those who did not have stickers.

And then she died. The warrior left the battlefield. In the church Doreen Bertrand left her scooter for a casket with wheels and "Amazing Grace" on a guitar.

Everyone cried.

After the service a couple of us went back to the parking spot. We watched a car with no sticker pull in, and we shook our heads slowly in sadness. The warrior was gone and the enemy would win.

But then something strange happened. We could see the driver looking up through the windshield at the Disabled Parking sign, and the car went back in gear and pulled out. It really happened. Someone simply did what they should do. Maybe the driver's eyes just happened to glance up. Maybe some departing spirit passed by and lifted the eyes. Maybe the eyes saw something—a finger wagging back and forth, a shadow, a tree branch. Something.

Probably not. No, of course not. We were there and did not see that.

But then again, we were not parked where we should not be.

You Got To Hate Someone

have friends who like baseball, and when they go to New York they want to see a Yankees' game.

"What a waste of money," I tell them.

I tell them to take the subway to Brooklyn and go to a low-income housing area and look at a plaque on a wall that says this is where Ebbets Field used to be. "That's where the Dodgers used to play. That's baseball."

"But they don't play there anymore," my friends say. "In fact, they haven't played there since 1956 and that was a long time ago."

"Doesn't matter," I say. "I hate the Yankees and love the Dodgers."

Let me explain. It was easy to hate them. They always won and we hated anyone who always won.

The Dodgers were human. They lost just like us. We lost in our street games. One team would get more runs than the other in stick-ball, which was our national pastime. A broomstick and a rubber ball—that was baseball to us. We lost in arguments with our parents, we lost in arguments with our teachers and we lost in games on the street. Not all the time. Sometimes we won, and that was human.

But the Yankees never lost.

We chose sides by shouting, "I want to be on Joey's side." "No, I want to be on Joey's side." In the end, half the kids were on Joey's side and half were on Jimmy's side, which no one wanted to be on.

Jimmy lived next to me, across the alley. We had a phone that was strung from one back window to the other, a length of string between two cans.

"Hello, can you hear me?"

"No, I can't hear you."

I have written about this before but it is one of the best memories of a lifetime, so forgive me if I repeat myself.

Jimmy had stuck his head out of the window and the string was slack. Of course he couldn't hear me. The string had to be tight.

"I can't hear you. You have to pull the string tight," I shouted out the back window across the alley to his window where his head was sticking out. We could hear each other fine without the string, so long as a train was not passing, which they did every few minutes. The train was seventy-five steps from our back windows. We counted. When it passed we couldn't hear each other even if we were standing face to face.

"If I pull the string tight I have to go inside, and my brother is sleeping," he shouted.

His brother had cerebral palsy and was like a six-month-old in his crib, except he was twelve years old.

There was another kid on our block with cerebral palsy. His name was Junior and he was Joey's little brother. Junior was better off than Jimmy's brother. He could walk, but it was very awkward and Joey ended up carrying him almost everywhere, which is why Joey was so strong.

But Jimmy's little brother spent his life in a crib, usually yelling or crying. And often when Jimmy stuck his head out of the window to shout to me I could hear his brother screaming from his crib. It was hard to be his next-door neighbour. It was harder to be Jimmy.

Anyway, half of us wound up on Jimmy's team and half on Joey's. We spent our entire young lives doing that and Jimmy's team would be called the Yankees and Joey's would be the Dodgers. We hated the Yankees. Everyone hated the Yankees.

There was a famous play called *Damn Yankees* that none of us had seen because it was a Broadway play, but we all knew what it was about.

It was written by someone from Brooklyn, we said. It really wasn't, but we said that because everyone in Brooklyn hated the Yankees. And in this play a fellow sold his soul to the Devil in return for the Yankees not winning the pennant that year.

The fellow who gave up his soul for such a good cause was named Joe. So we all wanted to be on Joey's team. You see, it all makes sense.

Everyone in Brooklyn, which is at the bottom of New York, hated the Yankees. The Yankees were and still are in the Bronx, which is at the top of New York. Anyone from the Bronx was bad, we said. Even though we had no money and the streets had litter and our fathers were in the bar, we said Brooklyn was good compared to the Bronx where everything was bad.

The people in the Bronx said the same thing about Brooklyn, which they said was dirty and poor and full of drunks. And besides, the Dodgers were in Brooklyn and they never won. The Yankees were in the Bronx and they never lost.

It is easy to see how prejudice is born. You just don't like someone else because they are from a different place.

And I repeat, the Yankees never lost. How can you not hate someone who never loses?

Every year they won the pennant, which means they were the best in their league. And then they went on to the World Series, which they won, no matter who they played. They were like Goodie Two Shoes in school who always knew the answers when the teacher asked the questions. Nobody liked Goodie Two Shoes either.

I don't know why we called him that. We all had two shoes, but that was all we had. We didn't have the answers, so we wound up staying after school while Goodie Two Shoes would go home at 3 p.m. You can see why we didn't like him.

This was the way life was meant to be. We were in Brooklyn with the Dodgers, whom we all loved, but they almost always lost.

They were called the Bums, the Bums from Brooklyn. It is hard to get respect when that is your nickname. The Yankees were called the Pin Stripers, because their uniforms had and still have pinstripes, like the wardrobe of someone who has tuxedos in his closet but no blue jeans.

The Dodgers did win the World Series against the Yankees once, in 1955. There was dancing in the streets and the *New York Daily News* ran a front-page cartoon of the unshaven face of a bum with a big open mouth with only one tooth, messed-up hair and a fat nose.

Above it was the headline: WHO'S A BUM!

It did not have a question mark.

Now that is real humanity. That is the way life is. You lose. Your friends lose. Everyone you know loses. And then you win, once. That is real. That is the way life is.

Later, when I got a job as a copy boy at the *New York Daily News*, I had to go to Yankees' games to carry film back to the newsroom. I had the best seat in the stadium, next to the writers and photographers. But it was the Yankees who were playing so I turned around and sat with my back facing them. No way was I going to let Joey down.

Hate is a powerful thing. Over all the earth there is no one else I don't like—just the Yankees.

Joey died last year. I still want to be on his team.

Again, the Photographer

"Cinema should make you forget you are sitting in a theatre."—
Roman Polanski.

Grant Faint headlines each of his photos with a quote from someone famous and deep.

Then he puts in his own words:

Krakow, Poland ... town square ... Polanski survived the WWII ghetto liquidation ... at the beginning of WWII there were 70,000 Jews in Krakow ... now there are less than 300.

It is a picture of a beautiful, ancient town square with market stalls below the old, stone buildings. The stalls are lit as the day ends. The buildings are dark. It is the kind of picture any tourists would love to take, but with Grant's words it has another meaning.

Seventy thousand Jews in Krakow; now less than three hundred.

Grant Faint is a photographer whom I wrote about several books ago. He was a news cameraman during my earliest days in television.

Grant was known for taking beautiful pictures and for being fearless. When the odds were against him and he was taking pictures of people who did not want their picture taken, he took their pictures.

And the pictures were beautiful, no matter whether they were of a criminal's face or a mountaintop poking through the clouds.

He began sending his pictures unsolicited to a stock photo company in New York. Since they were unsolicited, unasked for, unknown, they were rejected, one after another after another. But he kept sending them.

Then one day, while we were working, he stopped his camera van and dragged me into a newsstand.

"This, look at this," he picked up a major US magazine, like *Life* or *Look*. This was back when they were the *big* names in magazines, both for their wide readership and for the respect they had earned for their stories and pictures.

He opened the magazine at a cigarette ad, a full page, a major ad, the background of which was Grouse Mountain.

"That's my picture," he said.

After a few more sales, with his head full of dreams and totally confident that he could do this, he quit the television station and went off on his own with a camera and no other income. His wife was more than a bit frightened.

Grant had been through this before. When he was a boy and Christmas was a day away, the refrigerator was empty. "A church group came and filled it," he said. He doesn't know which group or which church or the names of any of the people who came with food. He only knows he will never forget that moment.

His new solo career gradually took off as he sold more and more of his pictures, boosted by the knowledge that he was good at what he did, and by the pleasure that photography brought him. More pictures turned up in magazines and billboards and on the cover of *National Geographic*. He travelled the world, spending much of his time in Africa and almost always taking one of his three kids with him along with any friend that the child wanted to take.

Many years passed. Decades passed. The pile of worn-out cameras grew. He took 70,000 pictures every year, which would turn even the finest camera into mush from exhaustion.

Over time his pictures brought him what would be considered by most photographers incredible wealth. It was not hockey-player wealth, but it was more than TV news cameraman wealth—somewhere very comfortably in between.

That is where the story ended the last time I wrote about him.

The New Chapter:

Then he wanted to fill someone else's refrigerator.

He used some of his income to help orphans in Africa. Then he gave more of his money. He made a motion picture of images in Africa and gave the entire proceeds from it to helping children in that continent.

He gave more, and built a school for 350 orphans in Sierra Leone. In 2010 he added a medical centre.

And still he wanted to do more.

Grant is now making a documentary, and it won't be his first. It will be called *Love Wins*, because, he says, in the end love wins every time. It doesn't hurt, it heals. It doesn't conquer, it allows all else, and then is there at the end.

He has learned this, I think, from his camera, and the title, as you will read, came from his work.

Grant sends a picture to me and about a hundred of his other close and personal friends almost every day. Sometimes it is lions in Africa, sometimes polar bears in the Arctic, sometimes clouds, but most often people, laughing, crying, playing or working.

One of the famous quotes he has used to accompany one of his pictures is from Winston Churchill: "Courage is rightly esteemed the first of human qualities because it is the quality which guarantees all others."

Then Grant added his own caption as he always does: "New Delhi, India ... the blind leading the blind at rush hour ... courage."

The picture shows three thin men in a line walking through traffic. The man at the back is holding the arm of the next man, who is holding the arm of the man at the front. Each one has a stick. The stick in the hand of the man in the lead is a white cane; the other two have sticks of wood—crooked, brown sticks.

That is courage. You can see that. You don't have to see the picture right now to see that. You can be blind and still see that that is courage. But when we are told eloquently by Winston Churchill and simply by Grant Faint, we more than see it. We know it.

I tell him he is a better writer than most writers I know. He is better than me. His only problem is he has no idea why you use a paragraph, or a capital letter, or a period.

Doesn't matter.

His writing, like his pictures, is art.

He sent a note to all his friends:

> today i am asking your opinion, feelings, thoughts, wisdom ...
> what is Love? what does Love mean in this world?
> if you reply i will give you my opinion arrived at after days of reading my collection of books,
> downloaded materials, poems, reviews of great thinkers men and women, and from all the great religions
> and quotes about Love.
>
> Grant

He spent months working on the concept. Some people work on ways to beat the lottery. Grant, an east-side kid, was looking for the meaning of love.

Then he found it. He sent a photo he had taken after finding some graffiti on a steel wall separating Israel from Palestine.

Much of it was in Hebrew, the rest in Arabic, but in the middle of a wall of writing that was unintelligible to a western reader were the words, scrawled in paint in English, LOVE WINS.

Grant is now going around the world asking people what love means to them, gathering footage of everyone from sheep herders to business leaders.

Then one day in Brazil he wrote:

The canadian photographer grant faint was MUGGED in busy part of buenos aires today

In broad daylight by two attackers. Mr faint is in buenos aires to record a sequence of tango dancing for his new film LOVEWINS a documentary about the state of LOVE in our world today.

Jumped from behind and tackled to ground Faint's injuries were slight however

He did lose a watch to attackers he had purchased thirty years ago when filming a five part documentary Series with well known canadian author McMIKE of Vancouver.

When faint was asked how he was he reacted by saying I love everyone just wish i had more to give to those poor people who are in such need they are forced to commit crimes such as this. I also

Wish I had a 9mm handgun, at the time this reflecting a state of his shocked mind.

Faint returned to his 5 star hotel and drank many beers ... the attackers who left on a waiting

Motorcycle are responsible for last month killing of a french

Tourist who was shot dead when he refused to give up his camera. true story

You see, Grant does not understand sentences, but he does know a hot news story. The next day he went on filming his sequence of tango dancers, and later he learned the dancers were in a part of town that had been the scene the week earlier of an attack on a British photo journalist.

The real punchline is that he continued on his search of proving Love Wins. That is better than moaning and saying it doesn't.

My favourite picture from Grant is of a beautiful woman in India. You can only see her back, but I know she is beautiful. She is wearing a sari of many colours. It goes over her head.

On her forearms are many bangles. On her head is a wooden plank and on top of that are ten bricks neatly stacked. I know there are ten. I count them every morning when I look at the picture. In her hands, with the bangles wrapped around her forearms, are two more bricks, one in each. She will balance and carry twelve bricks to somewhere and they will be taken off and she will walk back and get twelve more bricks. And in her beautiful dress with her precious bangles she will work all day and every day until she gets too old to work.

(Just for a joke, go out and try to pick up twelve bricks.)

And when each day is done she will go home and cook rice and beans and feed her family. And then she will clean the house and later, after putting her children to sleep, she may provide relief for her husband, relief that she will not get because of brutal customs that cut part of her body out when she was a girl.

All that is in one photo. That is what a good photographer does.

Above another picture he has copied a quote from Steven Spielberg.

"I dream for a living."

The photo beneath was taken in the New York Metropolitan Museum. It is the back of a nun whose body from head to foot is covered by a grey habit.

She is looking at two portraits of French Renaissance women

wearing intricately sewn, ornate gowns with low, revealing fronts. Each painting shows a smiling, seductive face with flushed red cheeks and the kind of look that says, "I am here if you are ready and rich enough and manly enough and self-confident enough to join me."

Grant's photo makes you stare at the motionless nun and say, "I wonder what she is thinking?" Is that genius or luck? Or both? Certainly one makes the other, always.

In all the years I have known him he has only sent me one picture he did not take. He said this one raises the problem with taking pictures: Do you interfere with what you see?

The photo is of a small, skinny toddler with her ribs pressing against her skin. She is lying on the barren ground somewhere in the Sudan. Behind the girl is vulture, waiting for her to die.

We don't see what happens next.

The caption under the picture reads that the photographer won a Pulitzer prize for this image. He killed himself two months later.

Photography is not easy. Not when it is deep and human. Not when you find images that can make or break a heart.

Living is the same.